tug of the current

The Red Moon Anthology
of English-Language Haiku
2004

Jim Kacian ✧ Editor-in-Chief

Ernest J. Berry ✧ Tom Clausen
David Cobb ✧ Dee Evetts
Maureen Gorman ✧ Carolyn Hall
A. C. Missias ✧ Kohjin Sakamoto
George Swede ✧ Max Verhart

© 2005 by Jim Kacian
for Red Moon Press
All Rights Reserved

Published by
Red Moon Press
P. O. Box 2461
Winchester VA
22604-1661 USA
redmoon@shentel.net

ISBN 1-893959-48-1

All work published in
tug of the current:
The Red Moon Anthology of
English-Language Haiku 2004
by permission of the individual authors
or their accredited agents.

Cover painting:
Nick Namarari Tjapaltjarri, *Bandicoot Dreaming*
1991, 71.625" x 59", synthetic polymer on canvas
Used with permission.

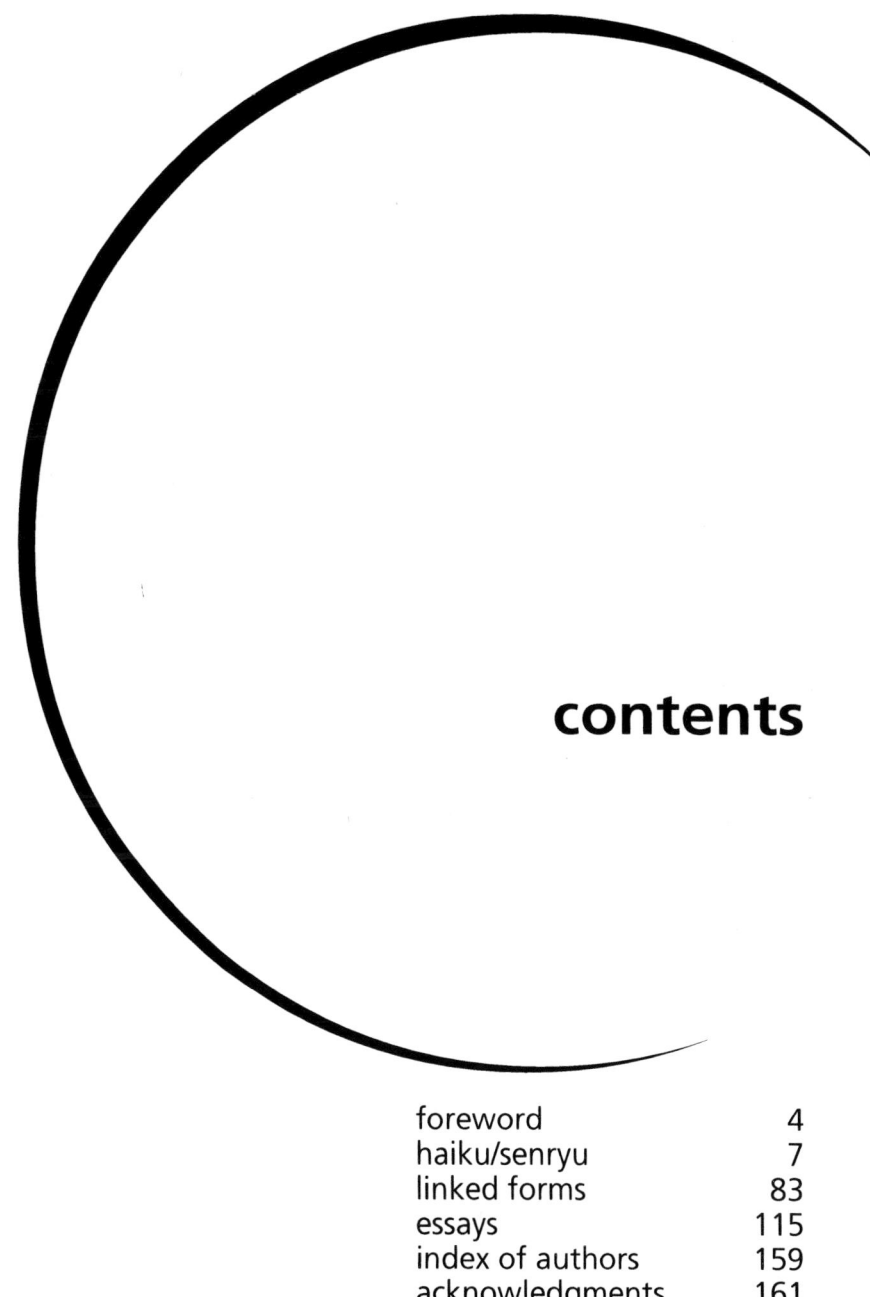

contents

foreword	4
haiku/senryu	7
linked forms	83
essays	115
index of authors	159
acknowledgments	161
sources	162
the RMA editorial staff	163
the RMA process	164

foreword

THERE IS AN OLD QUESTION which mechanics ask: how much of the car do you need to replace before it ceases to be the original car? If you change the engine, does it become something else? The transmission? Body parts? All the above?

An enterprise such as an annual anthology is a similar matter. Take, for instance, the circumstances of the editorial team: it is ideal to create a situation wherein there is sufficient turnover to present a fresh approach year after year, but not so rapid as to lose connection with the evaluation standards of prior years. So conceived, there is a track which a yearly product may leave, a smooth arc which may emphasize one direction or another over time, but no sudden departures from the general course.

I mention this because this volume's completion marks the departure of the last of the original editors of *The Red Moon Anthology*, Tom Clausen. The others who began this enterprise with me in 1996—Jan Bostok, Ellen Compton, Dee Evetts, Yvonne Hardenbrook, John Hudak, H. F. Noyes, Francine Porad, Ebba Story, and Jeff Witkin—have all moved on to other things over the last near-decade, though most of them remain quite active in haiku. We have missed all of them, and the talents they have brought to this volume. Similarly, we are favored to have our current crop of editors, who, too, bring different skills, tastes and interests to their considerations on behalf of this ongoing production. The result is a constantly shifting, yet stable, anthology which can be counted on to look carefully at the large bulk of haiku being published each year, and consistently select the top poems from among them, without bias towards a particular school or poetic. It is the editors' efforts, along with the poets', which has made RMA the annual event in the haiku community that it is, and without whom there could be no such volume. Thanks to all who have served and have made the first nine years of RMA so diverse and at the same time, so continuous.

Jim Kacian
Editor-in-Chief

tug of the current

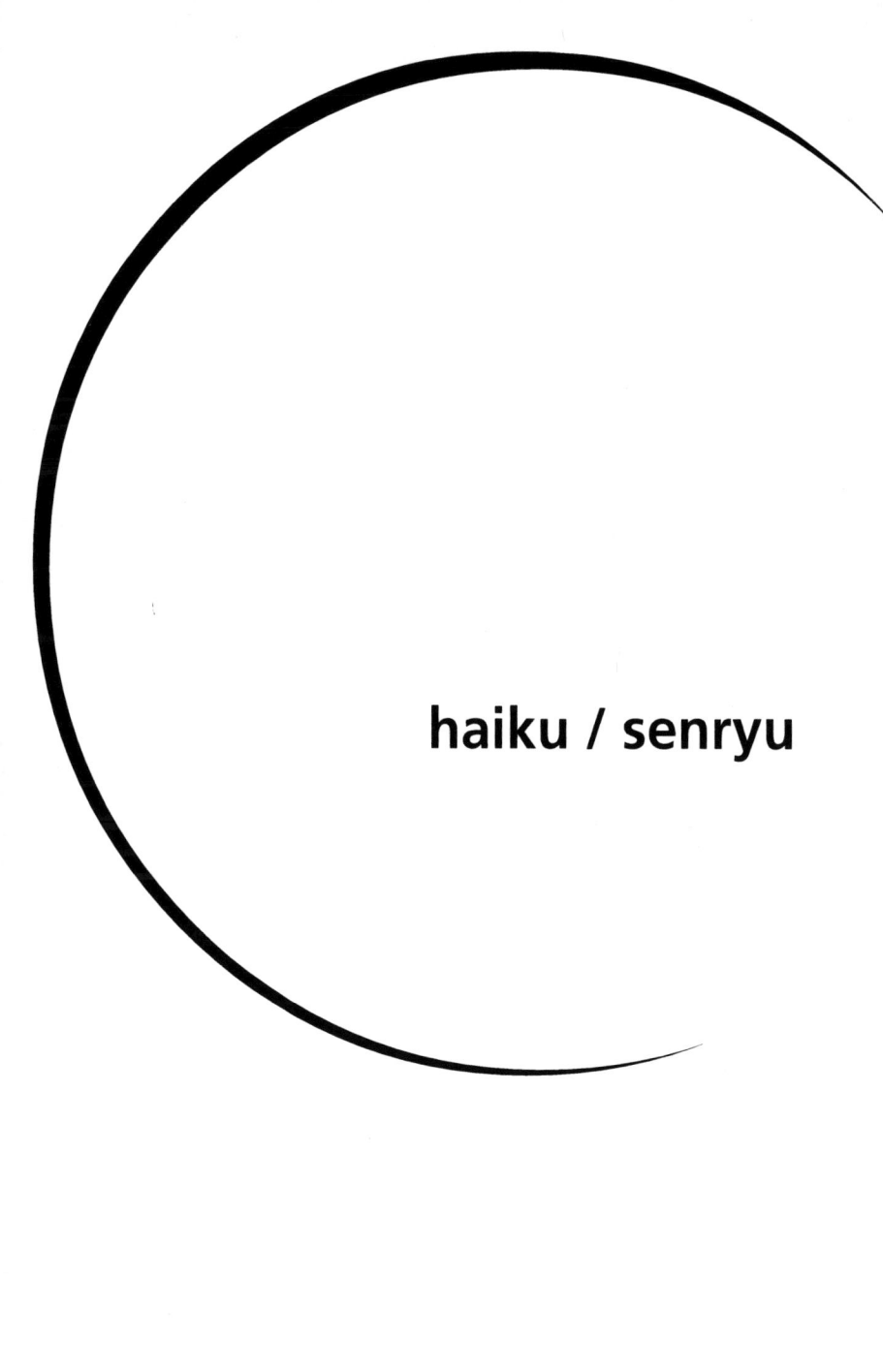

haiku / senryu

Stephen Addiss ✧ United States

reappearing
with each step in the snow
her red pumps

Stephen Amor ✧ United States

a field of crickets . . .
stepping in the spaces
between their songs

frances angela ✧ United Kingdom

garden party
light rain falling
into my mother's gin

backwards
into the falling shadows
the rower

Anthology 2004

Fay Aoyagi ✧ United States

a hole in my sweater
I ask him one more time
what he meant

Winona Baker ✧ Canada

office party
all the happy faces
on the balloons

Jack Barry ✧ United States

    a beaver's wake
    touches both shores
    first drops of rain

Louise Beaven ✧ Canada

    back at
    the antique shop to see
    what's new

Ernest J. Berry ✧ New Zealand

long eulogy—
the brother I never knew
I loved

2nd honeymoon
how nonchalantly
he pokes the fire

first light
a fly fisherman
catches it

John Bird ✧ Australia

    winter sun
    the guide points out
    celebrity graves

Michael Blaine ✧ United States

    moving day—
    watching the sun set
    somewhere else

Marjorie Buettner ✧ United States

a deep roundness
where the beetle burrows
summer solstice

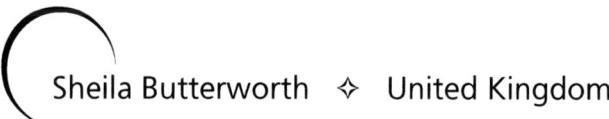

Sheila Butterworth ✧ United Kingdom

midmorning bus
no one young enough
to give up their seat

Yvonne Cabalona ✧ United States

dragonfly
the zigzag
of my attention

R. P. Carter ✧ Canada

around the war memorial road rage

Anthology 2004

Yu Chang ✧ United States

birdsong
my imaginary lover
alive again

xxx
am I
telling too much

The Red Moon

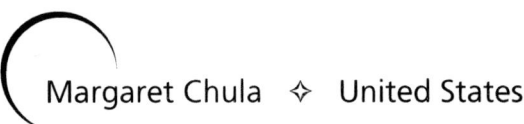 Margaret Chula ✧ United States

> end of summer
> the rust on my scissors
> smells of marigolds

> carrying moonlight
> into the house
> white peony

> war begins—
> my husband and I
> stop bickering

Tom Clausen ✧ United States

left and right
he follows the way
of his kicked stone

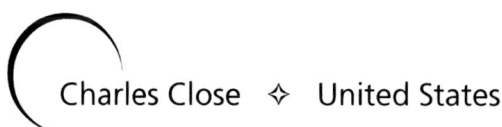

Charles Close ✧ United States

reunion photo
my long shadow
joins the family

Kathy Lippard Cobb ✧ United States

missing child—
yellow tape around
a field of violets

afternoon calm—
a bullfrog leaps
into its reflection

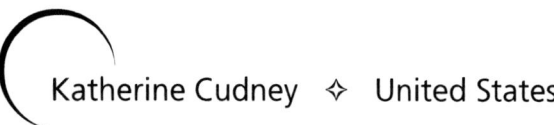

Katherine Cudney ✧ United States

a heart-shaped pebble
if you hold it just right—
our first days apart

a purple tree
when did I stop
being young?

William Cullen Jr. ✧ United States

Earth Day
the expiration date
on my bottled water

sand storm
the scorpion's stinger
aiming at the wind

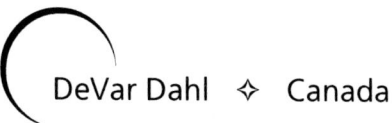
DeVar Dahl ✧ Canada

    the flat ends
    of a new pencil—
    first day of school

Anne LB Davidson ✧ United States

    beside the road
    feathers . . .
    enough for a bird

 Ian Daw ✧ United Kingdom

holding the ashes that once held me

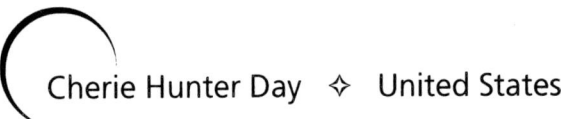 Cherie Hunter Day ✧ United States

hopscotch grid
faintly visible
first stars

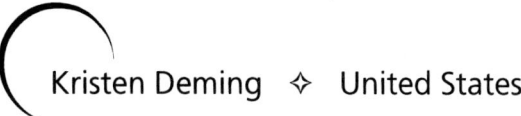

Kristen Deming ✧ United States

drifting snow . . .
lips of the newborn
suckle in sleep

Angelee Deodhar ✧ India

a child's haiku
not knowing when to stop
with the red crayon

Mike Dillon ✧ United States

    the distance between
    the hearse and the grave:
    spring rain

George Dorsty ✧ United States

    dead hamster—
    my son invents
    a religion

Connie Donleycott ✧ United States

summer garden
the full stretch
of the hose

creak of the swing . . .
my feet still reach
the sky

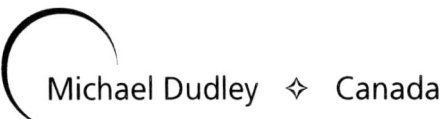

Michael Dudley ✧ Canada

deep winter t e e t h m a r k s in the borrowed pencil

Jeanne Emrich ✧ United States

Pleiades at dawn—
his hand comes to rest
on the small of my back

Robert Epstein ✧ United States

open window
the flutter of leaves
and post-its

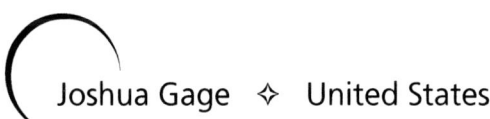

Joshua Gage ✧ United States

call from the hospital
a leaf caught in my wiper
leaves a streak

D. Claire Gallagher ✧ United States

breakwater—
the hush after
my opinion

Garry Gay ✧ United States

River stones
worn smooth
I have no regrets

 Barry George ✧ United States

    heat lightning—
    a second jackhammer
    picks up the pace

 Beverley George ✧ Australia

    lengthening shadow—
    above her eggs the hen's heart
    beats against my arm

Brian Gierat ✧ United States

> the corner
> where nothing grows—
> moonlight

Joyce Austin Gilbert ✧ United States

> after his death
> the too-ripe tomatoes
> on the vine

Anthology 2004

Ferris Gilli ✧ United States

        lakeside memorial
        the single shadow
        of clustered tadpoles

        hallowed ground
        the deep curve of a pine
        shaped by the wind

The Red Moon

Robert Gilliland ✧ United States

Valentine's Day—
a cyclist signals
with a long-stemmed rose

LeRoy Gorman ✧ Canada

cattle sold
all the gates on the farm
left open

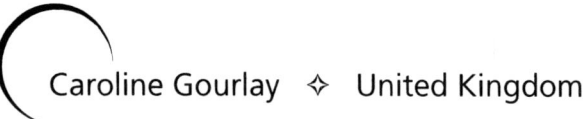
Caroline Gourlay ✧ United Kingdom

    eating in silence—
    the elongated fingers
    of the icon

Kay Grimnes ✧ United States

    cicadas
    none of the sawn boards
    even in length

Lee Gurga ✧ United States

midday heat:
the staccato staccato
of a nail gun

Carolyn Hall ✧ United States

slave cemetery
the tug of the current
on willow fronds

Anthology 2004

Timothy Hawkes ✧ United States

faint stars . . .
the cabby speaks
of home

Peggy Heinrich ✧ United States

half-empty bed
I try to recall
his faults

Christopher Herold ✧ United States

hothouse tour
a child sticks his tongue out
at an orchid

more deaths in Iraq
a flap of peeling birch bark
flutters in the wind

autumn sunset
the wake of a tugboat
sloshes ashore

Anthology 2004

Ruth Holzer ✧ United States

    gathering shells—
    I'm not
    who I was

Olga Hooper ✧ United States

    Monkey Year
    divorced again
    for the same reason

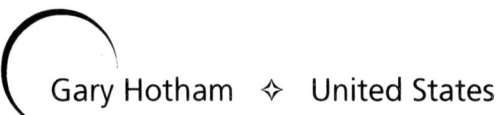
Gary Hotham ✧ United States

    the nail sinking in—
    my father's hammer
    in my hand

Vicky Houlder ✧ United Kingdom

    bright moon
    my shirt on the line
    stiffens

Kevin James ✧ United States

>late supper
>a sliver of moonlight
>on the cutting board

Tim Jamieson ✧ United States

>a ripple in the lake—
>something
>she just said

 Ken Jones ✧ Wales

    heavy evening
    from post to post the sag
    of rusty wire

 Jerry Kilbride ✧ United States

    year of the monkey—
    the hair in my ears
    grows thicker

Jim Kacian ✧ United States

lightning—
the fly resettles
in the same spot

a moment of doubt—
looking her in the eye
in the mirror

first warm day—
a tile reseats itself
on the patio

Karen Klein ✧ United States

      cold snap
      dog's pee on the snow
      closer to the door

Joann Klontz ✧ United States

      my lapsed religion . . .
      three flocks of geese
      waver into one

Deborah P. Kolodji ✧ United States

Christmas light test
trying to untangle
last year

Ekaterina Kunova ✧ Bulgaria

the bus station—
a frantic desire
for tenderness

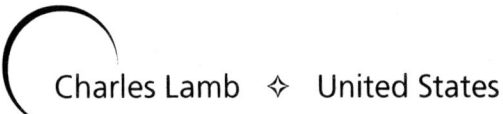 Charles Lamb ✧ United States

    nagasaki
    stone fingers reach up
    to catch the rain

 Burnell Lippy ✧ United States

    winter rain
    the shape of shoulder blades
    through her shawl

 Martin Lucas ✧ United Kingdom

a cloud of gnats:
the river's mood
eludes me

 Peggy Willis Lyles ✧ United States

the scent
of paperwhite narcissi—
an unfinished dream

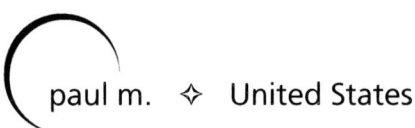 paul m. ✧ United States

       rain today
       a foot tapping
       of its own accord

       dusk . . .
       the awkwardness
       of the first guest

       Mother's Day
       a bit of shell
       in the chowder

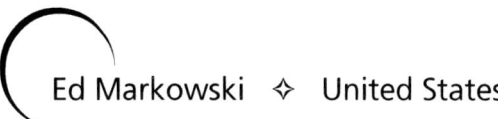

Ed Markowski ✧ United States

    december lay off
    the mall santa makes a promise
    I can't keep

Jeanne Martin ✧ United States

    dry riverbed
    it too
    leads to the sea

The Red Moon

Michael McClintock ✧ United States

>   a puppet taken
>   from the toyshop window
>   . . . winter rain

Dan McCullough ✧ United States

>   releasing
>   the pail of tadpoles
>   spring rain

Anthology 2004

 Allen McGill ✧ Mexico

> storm clouds
> the valley darkens
> farm by farm

 Dorothy McLaughlin ✧ United States

> morning commute—
> recognizing
> most of the strangers

Adelaide McLeod ✧ United States

the last words
of his epitaph,
untrimmed grass

Michael Meyerhofer ✧ United States

mentioning divorce—
rattle of a penny
in the clothes dryer

A. C. Missias ✧ United States

spring sun
the carriage horse shakes off
a cloud of dust

Emiko Miyashita ✧ Japan

early spring—
I sharpen the tip
of each colored pencil

Lenard D. Moore ✧ United States

hot afternoon
the squeak of my hands
on my daughter's coffin

Matt Morden ✧ United Kingdom

higher and higher
on the trampoline
spring rain

Marlene Mountain ✧ United States

the moon follows as far as i'm willing to go

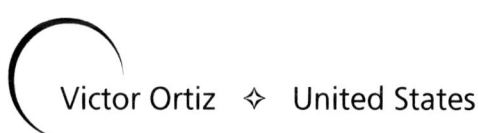

Victor Ortiz ✧ United States

suture scars along her spine pink panties

Pamela Miller Ness ✧ United States

autumn equinox
walking the loop trail
the other way

talk of divorce—
she leaves the map
open on her desk

birthday morning
he tells me that 53
is a prime number

 w. f. owen ✧ United States

longest day
the mower stalls
in high grass

summer dusk
the ice cream man
reaches deep

rain all day
my son flips
the etch-a-sketch

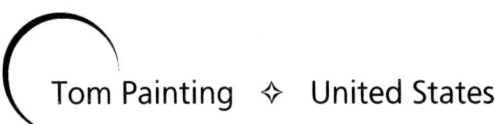 Tom Painting ✧ United States

paint by number
the child's river
escapes its bank

animal skull
the child fingers
her eye

peace rally
a forgotten scar
starts to itch

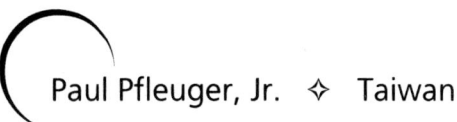

Paul Pfleuger, Jr. ✧ Taiwan

spring again
a taste of rust
in the harmonica

the heat
two boys take it
outside

Christopher Patchel ✧ United States

night train
we are all in this
alone

Alan Pizzarelli ✧ United States

the score keeper
peeks out of the scoreboard
spring rain

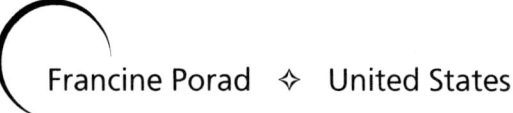
Francine Porad ✧ United States

inserting a piece
in my jigsaw puzzle
the TV repair man

Vanessa Proctor ✧ Australia

garden path
I walk through a gap
in the ants

The Red Moon

Lyn Reeves ✧ Australia

red sunrise
the bulldozer's engine
revs up

Dragan Ristic ✧ Serbia & Montenegro

this morning also
while shaving: in the mirror
there is an airplane

Chad Lee Robinson ✧ United States

Father's Day
the height
of the lighthouse

first frost
a slight dent
in the tetherball

Emily Romano ✧ United States

truant boys—
quarry depths
gather them in

Timothy Russell ✧ United States

spring rain
the gravedigger latches the door
of his backhoe

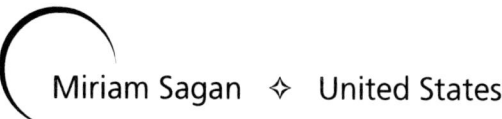

Miriam Sagan ✧ United States

    our exchange student
    folds paper cranes—
    Hiroshima Day

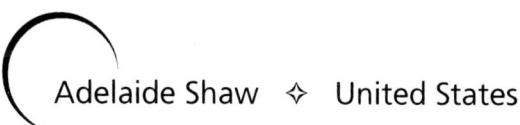

Adelaide Shaw ✧ United States

    a sudden warming—
    the snowman shrinks
    into his clothing

 Rob Scott ✧ Netherlands

summer's end
a boy skips a stone
to the other side

morning frost
your long absence
deepens

Anthology 2004

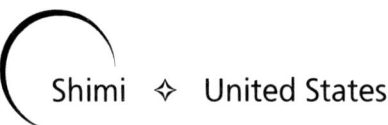
Shimi ✧ United States

    the crackle
    of a radio home run—
    Sunday siesta

Kuniharu Shimizu ✧ Japan

    holidays over—
    dry roses
    on the secretary's desk

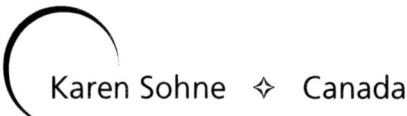
Karen Sohne ✧ Canada

>all that matters
>waving goodbye
>to the school bus

Sue Stanford ✧ United Kingdom

>hands in prayer
>the carpenter has one
>shorter finger

Anthology 2004

Alan Spence ✧ United Kingdom

rain on my birthday—
another year more
another year less

using a peach
for a paperweight—
summer breeze

John Stevenson ✧ United States

class reunion
everybody loved
my wife

fireflies
beyond
the sarcasm

Oscar night
adjusting the cuffs
of my pajamas

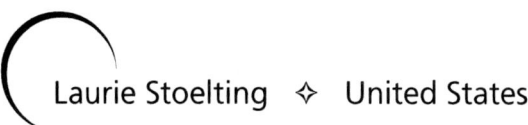
Laurie Stoelting ✧ United States

boat dock
we push away
the summer heat

a phoebe's erratic flight
this canoe trip
won't settle anything

Carmen Sterba ✧ United States

    single living
    I allow the kettle
    a full whistle

George Swede ✧ Canada

    Confessions over
    an old lady polishes
    both brass doorknobs

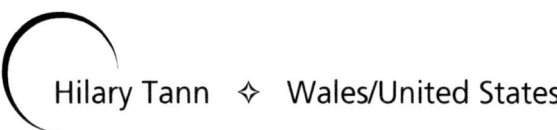

Hilary Tann ✧ Wales/United States

sitting
where I sat as a child
I wait out the storm

quietly
we become
audience

noh play—
watching the throat
behind the mask

Rick Tarquinio ✧ United States

> evening crickets
> star by star
> the dipper appears

Maurice Tasnier ✧ United Kingdom

> dressed again . . .
> just as though it
> never happened

Anthology 2004

Dietmar Tauchner ✧ Austria

a new year
the footprints
between graves

Tom Tico ✧ United States

my elbow slips off
the arm of the chair
autumn evening

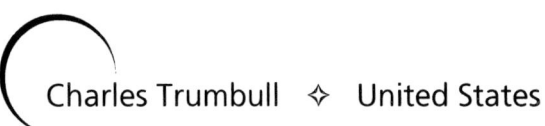

Charles Trumbull ✧ United States

sleepless night
from one end to the other
freight trains

here and there
over the battlefield
fireflies

Michael Dylan Welch  United States

tourists talking
in several languages—
the glassblower exhales

moving day—
the coolness on my cheek
after your kiss

morning chill . . .
the bag of marbles
shifts on the shelf

vincent tripi ✧ United States

    Fossil stone
       skipping it
          the same

Marilyn Appl Walker ✧ United States

late night sirens—
moonlight through the sheer
of her gown

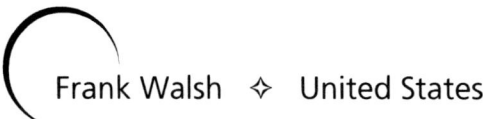
Frank Walsh ✧ United States

on display
her small and firm
opinion of men

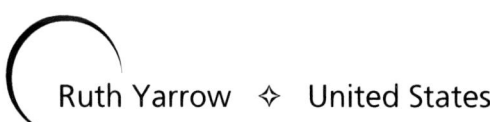
Ruth Yarrow ✧ United States

remote village
after the camera's click
her smile

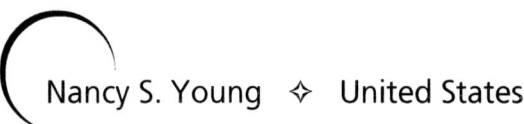

Nancy S. Young ✧ United States

    autumn wind
    in his sweater pocket
    the missing button

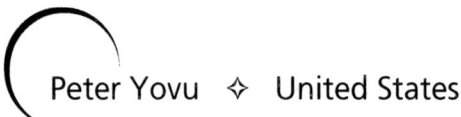

Peter Yovu ✧ United States

    leaves on the river—
    too old to call myself
    orphan

Cindy Zackowitz ✧ United States

autumn chill—
a butterfly swept up
with the leaves

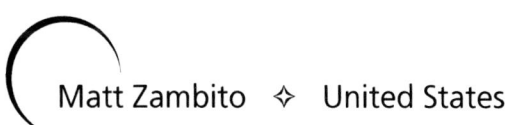

Matt Zambito ✧ United States

moving day . . .
the last pickle
floating in brine

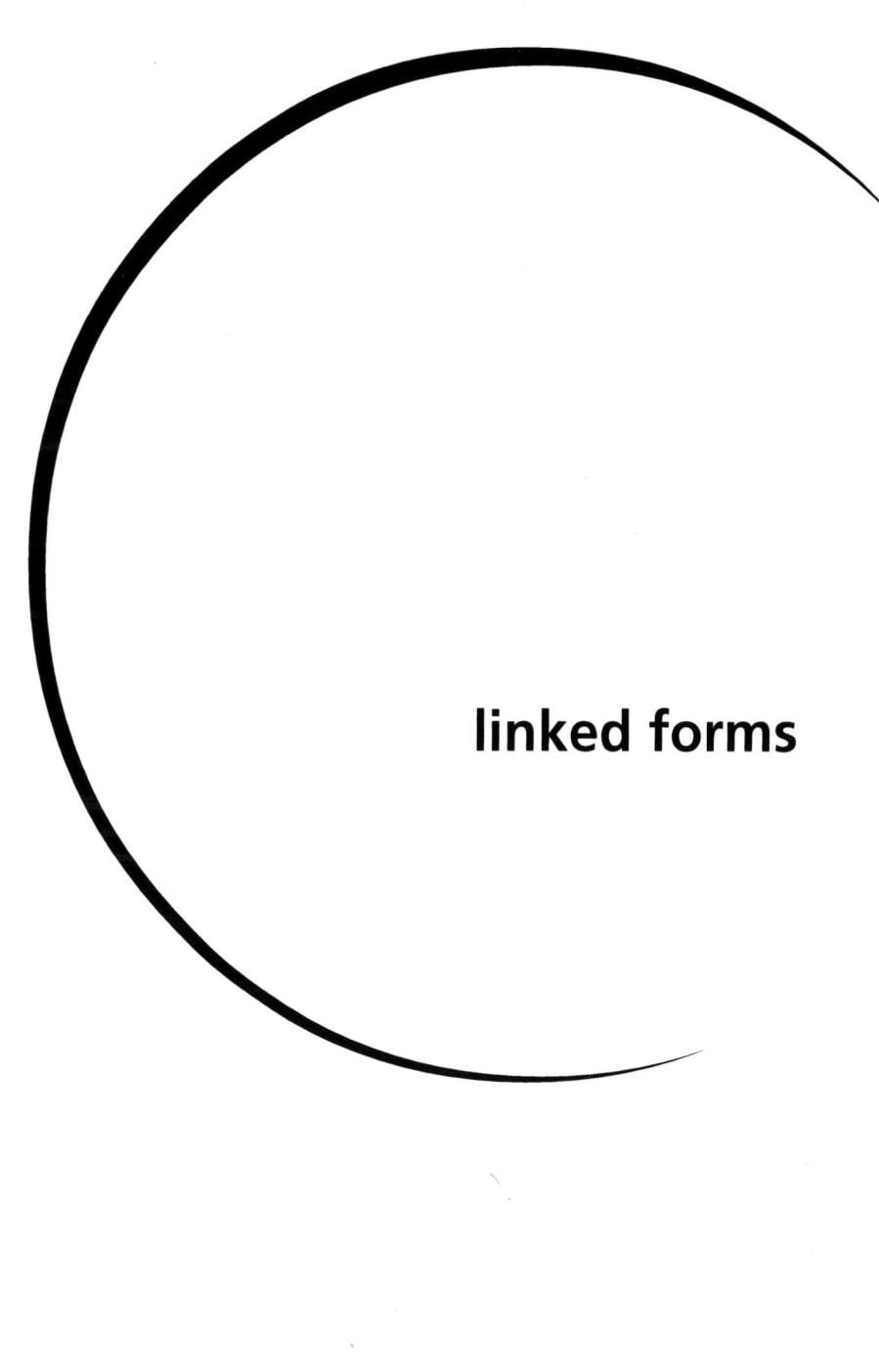

linked forms

Deb Baker ✧ United States

Embroidered Quilt

TWELVE PLAIN CREAM SQUARES, each a different month: a smiling snowman for January, nesting blue birds for May, a plump turkey for November, stitched by my mother's great grandmother in the wilderness of Ohio. She must have had so much to do. So why spend hours elaborately decorating? Scraps sewn quickly together would have been sufficiently warm. Once designed, what's left but the boredom: needle in, needle out, pull the thread, repeat? Was the repetition a comfort? An escape, a time to sit quietly and think? Was the quilt a gift for someone she loved, a child she was carrying? Perhaps she stitched for the same reason I write: so as not to forget.

        family quilt
        my daughter's fingers trace
        winter sun

Yvonne Cabalona ✧ United States

My Father's Daughter

SHE WAS MY HALF-SISTER. Raised by different mothers, I didn't know her very well. Occasionally I would search what pictures we had of her for any resemblance to me. Taken too young at 52 by a massive heart attack, the grief I felt was for my father. It was the second time I had ever seen him cry.

> early autumn
> the whiteness of the
> pallbearers' gloves

David Cobb ✧ United Kingdom

The Priest Hole at Oxburgh Hall

A WRIGGLE OF HIPS, a twist of the backbone, a lurch and you're down through the hole in the stone floor and into the brick-lined gut of the hide-away. You straighten up and sit on a narrow stone bench. You try to wipe something away, but it's a shadow and you can't. You think, Jesuit after Jesuit sat here and waited. Panic in their heartbeats, or faith in providence, if not the Pope? Salvation approaching at its own sweet pace.
 The walls sit tight as ever to this day.

> in a cobweb
> belonging to who-knows-whom
> a human hair

Hole with a View

> with a ball of string
> the sexton measures sunlight
> into portions

I CAN WORK OUT more or less where it will be. The "old half" of the village churchyard, downside of the bank which in gently undulating Essex is styled a "cliff," on the church side of the brook, admits no new corpses. Nowadays we of the village, when we are "spent," reassemble on the top shelf, in rigid sequence. Guess how many years you may have left to you, multiply this by the average number of burials a year (five or six), and this again by six for the allowance of feet per grave. You come up with a number that, using eye or boot, you can roughly measure to find out your final resting place.

    Mine won't be up teetering on the cliff edge, for that area is kept for leftovers of those who are cremated. A prime spot. Not because the cliff has any better sunshine, or is nearer the oaks and ashes where the songbirds gather, or closer to the bells that ring for weddings. Simply, it has the best view when the whole village, or most of it, come together on Christmas Eve for carols by candlelight. Passing between the worn headstones of the ancient squires, they slither for a little while along the greasy, grassy path, pattering the earth in which their forebears lie.

> how urgently
> the gardener fills the can
> with his own water

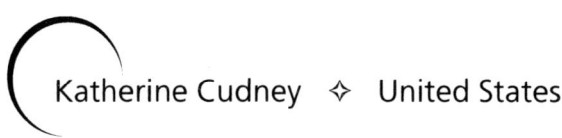

Katherine Cudney ✧ United States

Untied

WE FOLLOWED the orphanage housemother run down the corridor, single file. We were going to play indoors due to wintry weather. Waiting to enter the playroom, I stood in line in the required silence. Then it happened. After weeks of trying unsuccessfully to make a sound by blowing through my lips, a shriek escaped when I least expected it. The smack across my face was swift, but it didn't dampen my glee—I had learned to whistle! I smiled up at the wimpled face of the nun who admonished me. "But I can whistle!" I told her. She was not impressed and told me so before she slapped me again. I looked down at my feet, my face flushing from the heat of her temper. It was then that I noticed my shoelaces were untied. I looked at the heavy rosary beads hanging from the nun's belt and said a little prayer under my breath. She yanked me out of line by my ear, hissing that I'd have to sit out playtime until I tied my shoes. Never having learned to tie anything in all my four years, I spent the rest of the afternoon in the corner, flipping my laces, whistling softly.

> Ice-covered branches
> A wren breaks
> Into song

the weight of a sparrow

THE ORPHANAGE housed over two hundred boys and girls at any given time. My estranged parents' matriarchy convinced themselves that my older brother and sister and I would be happier living together in an orphanage than if we were divvied up between aunts and uncles. Ironically, the orphanage children were separated by gender and again by age, living in units quaintly called "cottages". The cottages were actually residential wings branching off a quarter-mile-long main corridor. The living quarters were of austere, concrete-block construction and painted a pale, institutional green. I entered the nursery cottage when I was two years old. After that, I saw my brother and sister only on visiting day, and then only if a relative had time on a Sunday to drive out and spend a few hours with us.

> heat lightning
> the weight
> of a sparrow

Each of the three nursery dormitories on the girls' side could accommodate up to twelve beds. I lived with thirty-five other girls ranging from two to six years old. We showered in groups of three or four, turning the water on and off in response to a verbal command given by a nun in full habit. She stood in the bathroom doorway, emphasizing her instructions by flipping the light switch on or off. Between the water-off and the water-on commands, we soaped ourselves thoroughly and awaited inspection, shivering from cold and fear of chastisement. A slap on a wet, soapy bottom always stung more when received in front of the others. After showers, we marched single file to our beds and knelt to thank God for a roof over our heads, food in our bellies and clothes on our backs. We also asked Him to take our souls in case we died while we slept.

        nursery rhyme
        the croak of a bullfrog
        from the murky pond

Lying awake in the narrow metal bed, I tried to remember my mother's scent. I rocked myself back and forth, the way I imagined she would if she were there with me. It wasn't long before I could feel the sharp stubble of my father's cheek against mine and smell his whiskey breath as he touched my face with goodnight kisses. Hot tears slipped from beneath my closed eyelids and I turned into my pillow, letting the floodgates open. The wrath of the housemother nun would have surely come down upon me if she'd been monitoring the dormitory intercom. I listened for her footsteps in the hallway, and, hearing none, I rocked and cried myself to sleep.

        storm clouds gather—
        the rustle of leaves
        startles a wren

Melissa Dixon ✧ Canada

The Conspiracy

AFTER MOVING to the Pacific coast from the east, I became aware of the open secret amongst those who reside near the ocean: at times of personal grief, islands and inlets on the shoreline are borrowed for private memorials. Illegal, yes, but on a windless day the sea doesn't care. The ancient womb takes back the contents of the humblest urn.

When the eldest son in our family lost his life on New Year's Day, it was our turn to conspire with the sea:

> a winter of waiting—
> first blossoms touched
> by frost

On a calm day in May, his sister, two brothers and I climb into a motor boat at the ferry terminal dock. My youngest son at the wheel, we head straight along the channel, mountains to the right of us, islands to the left. The motor roars; the boat vibrates; I hold onto the side with aching hands. Islands go by endlessly until cottages disappear. At last we cut the engine, gliding into the cove of a small, nameless island secluded by trees.

We all stretch with relief, inhale the salt smell of the sands, gaze beyond the cove. The channel here is wide as a large river and we marvel at the mountains opposite rising sheer from the water. At the same instant, we notice something unexpected: near us along the channel floats an immense flock of migrant seabirds. As far as the mountain! We can't believe what we see: "Hundreds!" "No! thousands!" The birds hold close together on the smooth seas—slender, soundless, sooty-black bodies. We watch in awe.

Finally we're aware of each other again. My daughter turns to me, seeking my hand for the long-delayed ceremony:

> his resting place
> a whisper of waves
> against the boat—

Four of us, each with different memories. We share words and silence. Tears follow ashes into the sea.

> the gentle tide—
> petals of wildflowers
> drift apart

When the sun's rays slant through the trees, touching our foreheads, we know it is time to go home. Emerging at low speed from the cove's entrance, we are once again struck by the sight of the seabirds still lining the channel to the foot of the mountains. They've drifted closer to us, the edge of the dense flock now a mere dozen feet from our boat. Bright eyes watch us watching them as we pass.

We accelerate slowly between them and the islands, the sound of our engine building. Suddenly wings move against water: the entire flock lifts in unison like a dark carpet. We're astounded! Seabirds are flying beside us, head-level—behind—in front. Seabirds are matching us speed for speed.

Along the channel their voices call back and forth. We answer—cheering, crying, laughing, waving deliriously. To our joy and amazement they stay with us mile upon glorious mile till dwellings appear. Then one bird rises, peeling off behind the boat—then another—more and more follow. We twist round in our seats to see them—streaming, soaring up and out, landing beyond our range on the open sea.

    Distance widens between us. Speechless, we shake our heads in happy disbelief, picking up speed for the ferry docks as light fades.

> sooty shearwaters—
> wings spread wide
> in the field guide

David Elliott ✧ United States

Independence Day

WHEN I CALL the nursing home after supper at 7:30 my mother says the girl had to wake her, sleep claiming more of her life it seems almost every day. After describing my Wednesday, I ask about the bill I'd received, the charge for two lunches—visitors she hadn't told me about? Was it Pearl? Someone from the church? "No," she says, "no one visited, it must be a mistake. But did I," she says, "tell you Earl was here?" Earl, an old family friend from the Midwest, surely would have let me know he was going to visit, and wouldn't his wife have been there too? "Write to him, will you, and ask if he was here. I have dreams so vivid they seem real. Often I can't tell the difference." After recalling her conversation with Earl—it was the 3rd of July—she asks if I remember the night in Indiana my great uncle Rea sprained his ankle leaving the fireworks searching for the car, and no I don't, but then the ghost of a memory perhaps appears—darkness and a ditch I somehow avoided falling into with him. We talk on, trying to agree on other 4ths of July. Had my uncle and aunt from Wilmington driven up with my cousins and had we really set off fireworks from the front porch? Nothing of that day returns but suddenly one of my 4ths rushes back. I'd just graduated from high school and a few of us decided to buy a watermelon and climb to the top of the quarry on the mountain where we could look out over the fireworks of so many suburbs in the New Jersey night.

> Spitting watermelon seeds
> off the cliff
> skyrockets exploding

Later Pete Lienhard surprised us by climbing up over the lip of the steepest face, Pete from Switzerland who years later died in an avalanche in the Alps, or was that only something I invented for a poem years ago? And then the 4th spent alone in an Ohio motel, hearing fireworks but not seeing them, on my way to a summer job in Minnesota leaving behind, it turned out, my girlfriend and probably my youth, this phone call reviving more memories, portions of the brain that light up with recollection, tiny fires that having been relit, will not die down as quickly and may be there the next time something opens a nearby door. But now, finishing the conversation—she wants to sleep—she asks when I'll remember to bring her those cashews she just asked for, you know, back in the spring.

> Above the fireworks
> steady
> evening star

Jeanne Emrich ✧ United States

Breath

I AM THE LAST in line. Up ahead, five spelunkers are on their bellies in a crawlway deep in the wilds of Mystery Cave, looking for a drop down into Cold Water Canyon. Falling further and further behind, I rely on muscles unaccustomed to such work straining to move the full weight of my body. Silently, I bless the spotlight on my hard hat. At least, there is a small, bright beam to light my way.

Now, everything seems to go awry. The battery pack around my waist loosens and moves around to my abdomen, just where it shouldn't be. Then the chin strap on my hard hat comes loose. I tighten it, only to realize with a shock that the ceiling is so low I can't even lift my head up to look around. A small panic grows in me.

"This is too close!"

Suddenly, I feel short of breath. I want to gulp, to make sure with each new breath that it is there and mine to have. Calling ahead to say I will stop and rest for a while, I let my body sink into the earthen floor. The wall is just inches from my face. I find the the deepest crack and peer into it, desperate for a feeling of space. All I can hear is myself breathing, each breath precious, each breath a gift. How intimate this exchange is, this simple, second-by-second give and take of air which I have always trusted, always taken for granted, until now.

        deep in the cave
        the earth returns
        my breath

Margarita Engle ✧ United States

Elementary Hindi-Urdu

THE WHISPERY LANGUAGE I studied so long ago has vanished. Only this one precious fragment of memory remains: I can still mispronounce and phonetically misspell *Santre bohut uchha he*, the oranges are very good. I've forgotten how to write an alphabet that dangles lovely loops under the lines of the paper instead of balancing them on top, but I do remember hands of prayer and the slightly bowed head, good oranges still a wonder worthy of reverence . . .

    sunlight's gold
      new fruit on old trees
      ripening

James Fowler ✧ United States

War

A NAVY MAN, a Nam and Storm vet, I'm long retired and newly wed. My wife and I visit Gettysburg. Through the slow beat of windshield wipers we peer out at the Virginia Monument, the North Carolina, Georgia, Arkansas, Texas, Alabama monuments. We look down on the Bushman Farm, the Slyder Farm.

> jungled coast
> a friendly-fire missile
> melts our main mast

We decide not to hike up, through the rain, to Big Round Top, but seeing the short distance to Little Round Top, we stop and go up. I read the plaques, circle the monument, look at the statues. I gaze down on Devil's Den.

> burning oil fields
> mask odors of desert heat
> carrier flight deck

We pass the Pennsylvania Monument, the Vermont Brigade. I get out and walk to the High Water Mark and stare out over the vast fields. The misty rain reminds me of cannon smoke. The Union soldiers, busy stopping Pickett's men, would have seen a similar sight. I cannot bring myself to step onto such blood-soaked ground. My wife takes my hand.

Cyclorama
"the next show starts in ten minutes
come see the battle"

I'm having troubles telling where the rain ends.

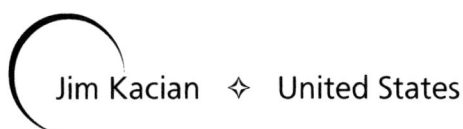
Jim Kacian ✧ United States

one main street

to the brief downtown—State Line, Mississippi—facades elaborated but without depth, a movie set, a western town set in the deep south

        noon on the hardpan—
        on the flat road the bump
        of an armadillo

by the Flat River

on a patchy day in September as i stop for breakfast on the way to New Orleans, love bugs at the first drops of rain in this droughty season begin to mate

        traveling alone—
        the smear
        of the wipers

mutatis

mutandi, new water flows and dispels the old, yet a boat does something deep which the surface cannot easily forget . . .

        calm morning
        the prow of the kayak
        splits the mountains

Nancy Tripp King ✧ United States

Washday

DADDY TENDED a four-acre farm with two mules and a plow. Ground-in dirt was a way of life, and looking decent, a daily worry to Mama.

> homemade lye soap—
> soot on the outside
> of the wash-pot

She scrubbed clothes on a washboard, her body bent, her arms doing all the moving. She had two tin tubs for rinsing.

> wash house
> the pump
> rusted red

She hung the clothes, sheets toward the road. On the back line, she hung step-ins, brassieres, and Daddy's threadbare long-handled underwear.

> flapping sleeves
> Slim Short's noon news:
> Madman on the loose

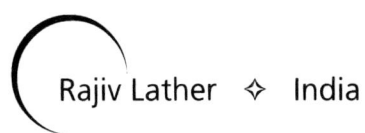

Rajiv Lather ✧ India

The Wait

IT IS A VERY HOT AFTERNOON with blinding sunlight and a bright blue sky. Parched fields, many of them overrun with dunes, radiate heat. Under a stand of banyan and bo trees, men smoke, play cards, and discuss the drought. Not far is the village pond, now shrunk in size, where teenagers bathe their buffaloes and take a swim. Camels lazily feed on tiny leaves of babul, their ploughs idle.

In the main street a long queue of women waits in front of the hydrant for the one-hour supply. They are dressed in long blouses over long skirts, their thin cotton shawls speckled with yellow, orange and red. Heavy silver jewelry, with a touch of ivory and gold, glitters around their ankles, arms and neck.

> sand whirls . . .
> in adobe shadows
> toy carts and rag dolls

There is a buzz down the line as water begins to flow. Women leave for home; balancing full earthen pots on their heads with the help of a thick cloth ring. As the hour comes to a close, a fight breaks out between the woman filling her third pot and the one behind her. It starts with an argument, moves on to shrieked abuses and ends in hair pulling. The supply shuts down and the two furious women leave empty-handed.

late summer dusk—
gossip
spreads faster than night

The next day, people gather in two groups. Meetings and lengthy discussions take place. Tempers flare as the temperature rises, and the situation becomes tense. The warring parties arm themselves with sticks and sickles to take over the faucet.

dark clouds—
the embers in hookahs
die out

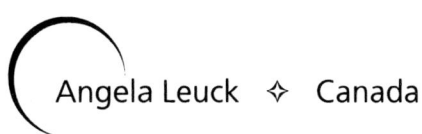

Angela Leuck ✧ Canada

Winter Morning

I WALK across a snowy field overlooking the St. Lawrence River. My destination: a red picnic table whose top has been swept clean by the wind. I sit and close my eyes to the glaring sun and flying ice crystals. In my down coat and scarf, I feel comfortably warm, as if I am in a cocoon, with no need to move, go anywhere, just breathe in the river air.

    decisions to make—
    only my own footsteps
    in the snow

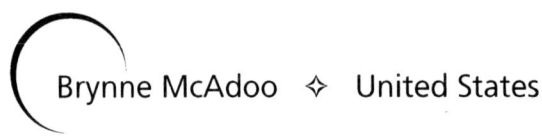 Brynne McAdoo ✧ United States

Haiku Rendezvous

I'S BEEN NEARLY A YEAR since I've seen him. I even moved, not leaving a forwarding number.

> you don't know
> where i live but still
> i leave the porch light on

Our phone conversation is short, nothing much exchanged except when and where we will meet, a secret spot: a cheesy cabin restaurant with an artificial fireplace. It is another place neither of us has been to and will never go again. I make sure I wear a black, fringed sweater he's never seen, a new shade of lipstick, Scarlet O'Hara Red.

I freeze in my heels when I see his profile at the bar, and he turns his face to me.

> his moustache gone—
> a shorter reach
> for our tongues

He voice steadies me, like it always has. The shabby, ordinary life I lead becomes poetry as we talk. Nothing else exists except his wide blue eyes and the worn little journals we each bring, scribbled full of our lonely love haiku. We take turns reading, each poem taking one slow breath.

> my haiku lover . . .
> not many words
> between us

I got worried about you when I wasn't seeing your work in *Plum Blossoms*, he says, his eyes like blue moons. Haven't submitted in a long time, I say, sighing. Maybe I needed you for some new material, I tease. He strokes my hair and plays with the ring on my finger. He writes something in my journal that I won't read just now. I can't tell you what the waitress looks like, though she fetches us drinks for hours. A married couple next to us listens in for a while and when they leave, we take their booth until the last call, and the waitress leaves the stark white bill on the table.

 It's cold out and I tuck my hand into the crook of his elbow as he walks me out, opens my car for me.

> after midnight—
> keys jingling
> in my door

Let's just stay a while longer, I say, though I didn't need to say it. As my lips find his, I know he is as imaginary as a lullaby and as real as a bruise. Later tonight, I will fall asleep, nestled in a dream of his arms. And tomorrow I will wake to an emptiness that fills every gaping, longing space within me. But now I do not care.

> the pull
> of my ex-lover—
> crater moon

Barry Sternlieb ✧ United States

Moonpath Cottage

CANOEING THE SHORELINE, we talk about our daughters, the future, the turmoil of news which seems very distant, and how good it feels to wipe the slate clean by simply focusing on oneness with the growth around us.

> quiet cove
> mating dragonflies
> light on light

Later we swim, our bodies so at home in this perfect water, it's hard to get out. Through the lazy afternoon, we nap in the hammock, read, and drink wine. The hours pass like reflections on waves. All day long, lake-living, the place gets into our blood, and we realize how each change is bound by quiet like the handsewn signature of an ancient book. So here is our hope for the end of the road: a tree-hidden two-room cottage right on the lake where one blue heron after another rows the sky in a slow steady rhythm returning us, cell by cell, to what seems forever unexpected.

> moonpath
> across the water
> a sudden kiss

Carolyn Hall (US)   ✧   Ebba Story (US)

Clack of the Rails

commuter train
tantalizing headlines
two rows ahead

a Valentine's Day bouquet
perfumes our trolley

uptown bus
the pickpocket so courteously
offers me his seat

leaving the station—
the conductor's ticket punch
glints at her waist

from the knapsack in his lap
a muffled meow

clack of the rails . . .
meadowlarks on a fence
whisk past the window

Carolyn Hall (US) ✧ Billie Wilson (US)

Lingering Light

alfresco art class
clouds sweep across
every canvas

lingering light—
the nude model's charcoal smudge

a chalk outline
on the asphalt—
hot summer night

thin moon—
an unfinished sculpture
gathers dust

Venus in Aquarius—
her mood darkens

street signs
blackened with graffiti—
we drive toward the dawn

William J. Higginson ✧ United States

The Small Hours

the small hours
a sudden dampness
of spring rain

spring colds
her snoring eclipses
my labored breathing

the spring night
an empty commuter train
streaks to its suburb

the spattered window
haloes a distant light
spring melancholy

a silver maple
looms in the night sky
its tiny blossoms

the soft night
a cough from one apartment
then from another

April night
raindrops go pattering
between my thoughts

Michael Dylan Welch (US)   ✧   Brian Tasker (UK)

On Broadway

another birthday...
overpriced cheesecake
at the neon-lit diner

the rapper's sneakers
flash at each step

red light—
a streetwalker whispers
hello there . . .

Club 69—
the stretch limo
turns on a blinker

drunken girls
waving glowsticks

a taxi home—
Broadway lights
dimmed for Hepburn

New York City, 2 July 2003

Michael Dylan Welch (US) ✧ Ikuyo Yoshimura (Japan)

The Hilltop Castle

autumn rain—
the blurred view
from the hilltop castle

umbrellas sold out
a shower of cherry blossoms

distant siren . . .
an unexpected drizzle
mists my sunglasses

thunderstorm—
a dog's black coat
steaming

cloudburst ends
the little girl's tantrum

rainbow
over the meadow
where we used to picnic

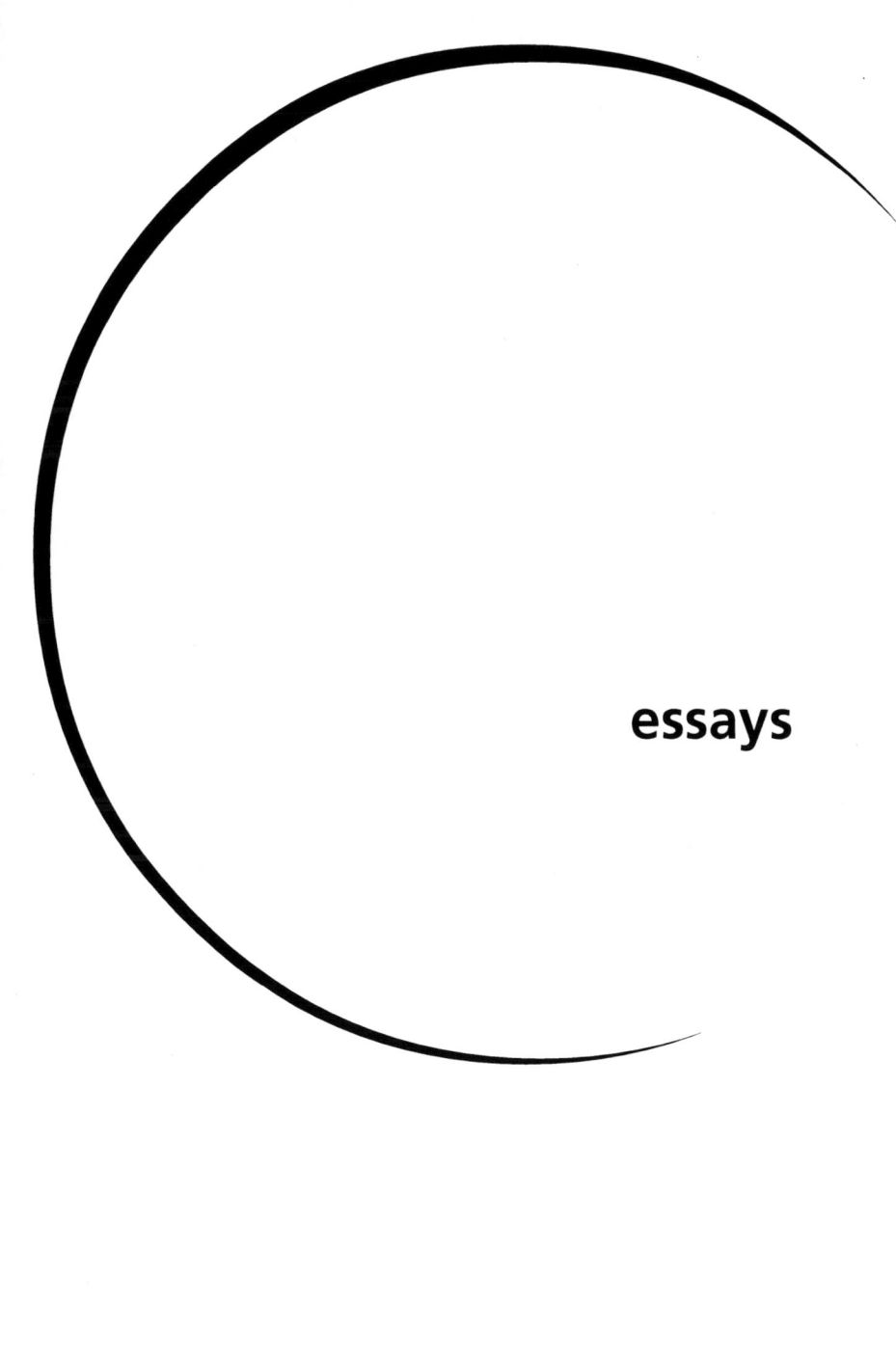

essays

Efren Estevez ✧ United States

Images of John Wills

THIS IS AN EXAMINATION of three haiku of John Wills, focusing on the images he uses and the way these images are portrayed. Wills writes like a painter of *sumi-e*. His depictions are monochrome, drawn with the fewest of brushstrokes, each line carrying great weight, not only in visual terms, but also in terms of the overall tone and meaning. This visual spareness conveys the beauty of the natural world in a mood of simplicity and solitude.

> first light
> between the snow and snow
> the pencilled woods

Dawn is breaking in a snowy landscape. The woods, which separate the snow, are "pencilled," emphasizing that the trees are bare and gray. It is almost a geometric design, with gray and white shapes contrasting and separating each other. Dawn is associated with color usually, such as rose or yellow-orange, but not here. This light is the very first light of morning, illuminating the scene in the midst of darkness. The woods and snow are just being revealed by the light. Thus the dawn light too is a shade of white and gray. In fact, the whole image is monochrome. It could be drawn only with plain pencil. The haiku reflects the aesthetic of wabi or poverty. Instead of an effulgent, glorious dawn, we have an understated, modest hint—just the very beginning of day, sketched with the barest number of strokes.

The metaphor of a work of art, here a pencil drawing, suffuses the poem. Pencils are made of soft carbon—graphite—which could suggest an earthy solidity to the woods. In order to draw the snow, however, one needs only the outlines. The snow itself can be the blank parts of the paper. It is an absence. Snow has traditionally depicted the transient and ephemeral because it melts away to nothing. The penciled woods define the boundaries of the snow. They separate two blanks.

The word, "pencilled" brings a human element into the scene (a British spelling is used, rather than "penciled," the one more familiar to U.S. readers). The woods seem to be drawn in pencil by a human hand. But the poet is not looking at a picture. He is looking at a landscape. "Pencilled woods" is a metaphor. The woods appear as if pencilled. The poet is not looking at a drawing in a book; he is seeing nature, experiencing it at a particular moment. The image is seen as a work of art. What "artist" drew nature? It is as if the original Creator just drew the woods there on the first day. "Between the snow and snow" has a Biblical cadence. Note in Genesis— "And God said, 'Let there be a firmament in the midst of the waters, and let it divide the waters from the waters.'" "Between the snow and snow" sounds like "divide the waters from the waters." And "first light" suggests "Let there be light." It is not just any time during dawn; this is the "first light." This lends a pale glow to the scene as mentioned earlier, but there is also the implication that this is not only the first light of a particular day, it is the first morning of the world. Perhaps in this sense the poem is paying homage to the original artistic act.

>blackbirds
>on the blowing reeds
>one above another

This is another image that can easily be pictured on a scroll or a screen. Blackbirds weigh a little over two ounces, light enough to be supported by reed stalks. The lightness of the birds and the surprising strength of the reeds are a source of pleasure and wonder.

The breeding season for blackbirds is summer, when they congregate in freshwater marshes or swamps and nest in the reeds and cattails. Since the wind is blowing, perhaps it is late summer.

Looking at the visual aspects, Wills identifies how the birds are positioned ("one above the other") both in regards to each other and within the picture frame. A view of two, or perhaps more, blackbirds is arranged artfully on the reeds. A seemingly random moment of the natural world is ordered and beautiful.

> a dog fox barks
> the snow lies deep
> in the hills

For foxes, mid-winter (December and January) is the peak mating season, so they roam while seeking partners. Cubs that were born in the spring are chased away by the parents and forced to make their own way. This activity results in territorial barking by other, already established foxes.

This barking imbues the poem with loneliness. It is a single fox, alone, barking. In this case, the primary sensory involvement is auditory, not visual. The barking is the only active detail in the scene. Perhaps the barking is muffled—both by distance and by snow. The line "the snow lies deep" conveys a sense of the world being covered and withdrawn, reinforcing the *sabi* of the poem. It is interesting that the detail provided about the fox lets it be heard, but not seen.

The visual image is an empty landscape of snow

in the hills. The world is still, but for the barking of the fox. Ironically, this sound draws attention to the silence of the scene, which, interestingly enough, is portrayed in visual terms instead of auditory. Silence is expressed by the image. The lines "the snow lies deep / in the hills" is a "quiet" visual image, the exact opposite of the barking auditory one. While the two earlier poems dealt primarily with visual images, this one does something more complex. It combines an auditory image with the visual. These two images balance and contrast each other. This is a scene both frozen and lonely, but also deeply calm and beautiful.

There are examples of this visual trait in other haiku of John Wills. The effectiveness of his images and the artistic perspective he brings to them is striking. Much more could be said about each of these poems from other perspectives. I hope the present essay promotes more discussion about his work.

John Wills died in 1993.

Dee Evetts ✧ United States

The Conscious Eye: Urban Haiku

THE SUBJECT OF URBAN HAIKU has generated a considerable response, and once again my post-bag has provided an angle of approach for this column. Letters from Michael Ketchek and Paul Miller offered some thought-provoking observations, along similar lines but with different emphases. Here first is Miller:

> I think haiku's purpose like most of Art is to allow mankind to unite—albeit briefly—with a loftier world from which civilization and its machinations have long since been estranged. Thomas Hemstege put it well in the latest issue of *Modern Haiku* when he said, "The object is to find something in nature that will accurately reflect that particular mood of the moment, a leaf, a cloud..." But why nature? I think this is because nature has a cycle that can be easily translated to our own cyclical moods—from the joy and hope of Spring to the acceptance and perhaps bleakness of Winter. Nature is an easy metaphor. The City, however, does not have such cycles. It is a machine that acts the same in Spring as it does in Winter.

The Hemstege quote is unfamiliar to me, and I find it quite startlingly reminiscent of T.S. Eliot's proposal* for an "objective correlative". But why

---

* 'The only way of expressing emotion in the form of art is by finding an "objective correlative"; in other words, a set of objects, a situation, a chain of events which shall be the formula of that particular emotion; such that when the external facts, which must terminate in sensory experience, are given, the emotion is immediately evoked.' ("Hamlet and his Problems", 1919) indeed must this be found in nature? Could it not equally well reside in a human gesture—let's say, the pose of a mannequin in a store window, the way a shoe-shine boy flourishes his rag, or a Japanese commuter bows to his fellow-passengers upon boarding a train? We may readily agree with Miller that the rhythms of the natural world reflect our own emotional cycles, endowing them (often consolingly and holistically) with a larger context. But is it really the case that the city does not have such cycles? My ten years as a New Yorker suggest otherwise to me. And it is not difficult to find poems that demonstrate the effect of the seasons on a great city. Here are four from among many:

> first snow
> brought in from the suburbs
> on the neighbor's car[1]
>
> summer heat—
> the nightlong buzz
> of a streetlamp[2]
>
> public garden
> she photographs the iris
> I just smelled[3]
>
> spring thaw
> the young cop aims
> her snowball[4]

These, in order, are by Doris Heitmeyer, Christopher Patchel, and Bruce Detrick, while the last is my own.

On reflection, I take Miller's meaning to be that the city does not *of itself* have such cycles. Certainly this seems to be the drift of Michael Ketchek's comments:

> One of the problems of urban haiku is that very few urban images are archetypal and therefore [are] unable to stir deep emotions in the way that images from nature or a more pastoral setting do . . . Besides the lack of archetypes there is another major obstacle to writing urban haiku. In haiku, through its use of juxtaposition, there is an underlying feeling of the interconnectedness of things . . . Urban life can be seen as the opposite of this expression of the connectness of things . . . as alienation from the earth and the natural cycles of seasons and life and death.

If this is the case, could it be that a deep-seated impulse to resist this alienation is precisely what drives so many city-dwelling haiku poets to observe and to celebrate natural cycles, wherever these push their way through or in between the mechanical, the commercial, the digitalized?

From this viewpoint, such poems are to be seen as vital and authentic expressions—rather than representing a nostalgic hearkening after distant realities, or an idealized notion of what subjects are appropriate to haiku (both of which have been frequently suggested).

I stated earlier that we can easily find poems that show the effect of the seasons upon the urban environment. It may then be more accurate to say that it is the *citizens* who are affected, despite the insulating tendency of the city. And at a profound level it may be that we want and need to be thus affected, to feel the connections, to take note of and take satisfaction in the first roller-bladers in the park, the roar of traffic recalling a recent vacation near the ocean surf, or a businessman taking a short cut across a frozen pond.

I have selected another half dozen poems that seem to exemplify this particularly well:

bridge traffic
moving slower
than the river[5]

at the market
the spot on the melon
where it lay in the mud[6]

afternoon sleet
cathedral door
unlocked[7]

Central Park sunset
a man with a briefcase
crosses the frozen lake[8]

vacation over
hearing the sea
in the traffic's roar[9]

summer rain
the bank teller shares
his peanuts[10]

These are by: Joann Klontz, Cor van den Heuvel, Mike Dillon, Doris Heitmeyer, Pamela Miller Ness, and Mark Brooks.

I find the image of a river, flowing as it does through so many of the world's great cities, a potent reminder of the larger and more permanent forces that we tend to regard merely as a backdrop to our elaborate constructions.

Klontz's bridge also brings to mind another of Ketchek's remarks:"This is not to argue against urban haiku, or to say that there are no aspects of urban life that are part of the collective unconscious. Certainly skyscrapers are symbolic of humanity's secular aspirations, in the same way as a steeple represents western religious goals."

I have on this occasion side-stepped the question of whether human activity is as much part of "nature" as that of any other species. And by extension, whether our connections and relations with each other are not simply another aspect of the larger connectedness discussed above. Next time, I will attempt to address this, while examining poems—*grittier* work, some would say—that reflect some of the more intrinsically urban scenes and interactions.

*   *   *

1. *New Cicada* 10:2
2. *Modern Haiku* 33:3
3. *For a Moment* (Farrington Press, 2000)
4. *endgrain* (Red Moon Press, 1997)
5. *Bridge Traffic* (Tiny Poems Press and Winfred Press, 1998)
6. *After Lights Out* (Spring Street Haiku Group, 1996)
7. *Modern Haiku* 34:2
8. *The Pianist's Nose* (Spring Street Haiku Group, 2001)
9. *ibid.*
10. *acorn* 5

Jim Kacian ✧ United States

Looking & Seeing: A Study of Haiga

OF ALL THE CONTRIBUTIONS to world art to have come from the Japanese, haiga is the most unique. It is, by definition, a combination of visual and verbal elements which work in ensemble to create an aesthetic experience quite distinct from either element taken by itself. This combination of pictorial and poetic materials is rare in any culture, and especially so in so-called "high" culture: besides haiga, other such combinations would include comic books, captioned drawing (most often humorous), posters, print and television advertising, calligraphic art, the work of a very few western artists such as Roy Lichtenstein, graffiti, and not very much else.

Which is perhaps surprising when we consider that the visual and the verbal are the two most powerful and frequently employed elements of communications. Or perhaps not surprising, since each is so powerful in its own right, and so demanding of attention, that it can be ineffectual to combine them; similarly, perhaps the overlap between the two might be considered a distraction from either. Whatever the explanation, there is very little history to such a combination in art.

All art has a set of conventions which the audience must know in order to appreciate the work. It is in the acquisition of these conventions that we decide if a work is "accessible" or "difficult". When the art form is combinational, then a combinational set of conventions must be employed, and this is part of what makes these works function, and part of why they can be hard to grasp. Let's consider some of these forms just to see what the artist and/or author has done, and what his expectations might be.

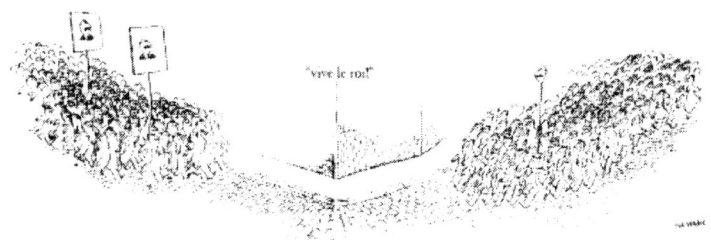

In the first sample, a political cartoon by Sempé, note how the convention of reading left to right makes it possible to "get" the joke; presumably if the head featured in this cartoon was Chinese, the "poster people" would be on the right side of the panel.

The second sample, from the comic strip "The Adventures of Phoebe Zeit-Geist", written by Michael O'Donoghue (later a writer for *Saturday Night Live*) and drawn by Frank Springer, and published in *Evergreen*

Review in 1962, employs a figurative means of distinguishing speech, say, from narrative. Do we all know how to read these? That is, is the order apparent? How did you know? It is apparent, too, from these cels, that the artwork from panel to panel may be discontinuous. Multiple angles and views reflect the influence of cinema.

In the third, a poster from the Russian Revolution by an unknown artist in 1919, the power and orderliness of the text is underscored by the horses, symbols of domesticated power, brought up to the mark by their human riders. "Mount your Horses, Workers and Peasants!" the poster exhorts, and the unity of the "goal" is seen to be compelling enought to unite horses and even men of decidedly different breeds and ethnic origins. A powerful message in a brief compass.

Another combination of text and art is calligraphic poetry. Depending on the work in question, these may feature the text, or the image, or find a balance between them. This example is Apollinaire's "Il pleut" translated by Oliver Bernard and retaining the shape of the original. What's particularly of interest here is that this is a typeset shape poem, unlike most, which are hand-calligraphed. Apollinaire was taking advantage of some new advances in typography which make precise position simpler to do. In this instance, the text is supported by

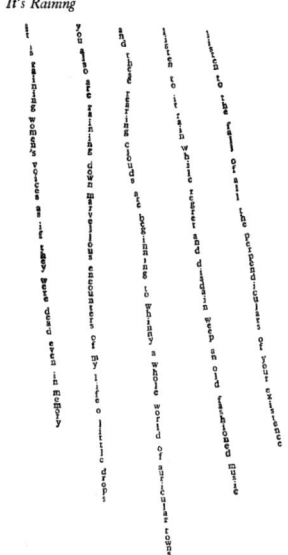

It's Raining

the typography, and while it could stand in a more typical stanza-ed format, it is clearly enhanced by the present treatment. And perhaps we could allow that the art herein presented might stand on its own, but admittedly it would be fairly meagre.

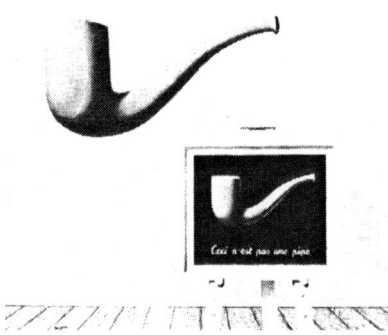

This fifth image is a deliberate attempt to utilize text as a focal element within painting. Magritte's "The Two Mysteries" intentionally blurs the line between that which represents, and that which is represented. There have been many other analogs in other arts: John Cage's *4'33"* during which the audience participates in a musical "silence" leaps immediately to mind. In the present work, this painting relies upon the written text for much of its "import", and as such is as much about reading and interpreting as it is about assimilating visual information. Which is both like and unlike haiga, as we shall discover.

The degrees of abstraction utilized in all of these examples is considerable. None attempts a formal realism. All rely upon the audience's willingness to grant "artistic license" to the illustrator so that the point might be made the more quickly. We do not pore over the drawings, or even the painting, as we might over a painting which intends to realize its full intent through strictly visual means. All of these rely upon our translating the events into sense within ourselves, unlike, say, a Rothko, where the intent is clearly non-informational, at least on the verbal and cognitive level. Here we are invited to dwell in the emotional waters of color, and no "interpretation" on a verbal or rational level is needed, or sought. Compare this (admittedly extreme) example to the other work we've looked at. In the cartoon, there is a predominance of interest in the visual aspect; in fact, we could do away with the text altogether. It functions rather as a caption, a tag with which to handle it. In the comic strip there is a more equal emphasis, with the verbal element carrying forward the narrative and the drawing adding richness and often humor and sexuality to what would otherwise be rather dry and insipid dialogue (in fact, it is the juxtaposition of these elements that make for the particular appeal of this strip). In the poster, even the convention of depth is subjected to a powerful stylization, and the text is an explanation of the image as a commentary, quite outside its visual interest in its own right. The exhortation would seem rather sterile without the power of the graphic, but the graphic holds interest on its own. So again, the verbal element could easily be excised in this case, but is not because the painter needed to make an intellectual point quite beyond the visual information already supplied. In the Magritte, the text sets up the parameters, the conventions, if you will, of how the picture is to be understood: that is, as an intellectual conundrum, as all art is. And in the Apollinaire, the one informs the other, while not being totally dependent upon it.

We might further consider the combined art and text used in advertising—"It's the real thing" accompanied by a swirl of color, suggestive of a wave, is a good instance. These often attain a level of artistic interest, but it is clear that their intent is not this beauty, or at least not primarily, but rather, an appeal for quite other purposes. I have not, as a result, included such work here.

Nor do I consider captioned photos beyond this brief note. The intent of such work clearly is to have the one explain the other. There is no particular expectation that they resonate, but simply share information which is being transmitted.

What about haiga, then, in this context? What does haiga attempt to do, and how can we link it with the tradition of combinatorial artforms as we have just explored?

I think it is apparent that none of the examples we've looked at function precisely as haiga does. The humorous drawing, at least in this instance, could have dispensed with the text. However, many cartoons do exhibit an interdependency between visual and textual material, and as such it is perhaps closest to haiga. But even here there are some differences. Most cartoons are humorous, and the text is arch: the intent is not resonance, but irony, and intellectual humor. So perhaps we would consider cartoons more akin to senryu, and perhaps we should imagine a new form of haiga, perhaps to be called senga, which treats this sort of material.

The others share some points, but lack others. For instance, the comic strip has a balance of interest between visual and textual elements, but features narrative, which is clearly outside of the purview of haiga. The poster is hortatory and hyperbolic, whereas haiga, at least as it has been practiced traditionally, is usually understated and seductive. The Magritte aims rather toward the intellectual than emotive or intuitive, and as such is perhaps more linked to philosophy than to art. And the calligraphy art, at least in this case (and in virtually all others I know) must seek to balance clarity with visual verve, a difficult feat to attain. So haiga's uniqueness remains, partially due to its unusual juxtaposition of art and text, and also partially due to its intentionality.

It is this intentionality that I wish to explore, and specifically how this intentionality informs the conventions by which we interpret it, as well as the parameters by which we create it. As haiga becomes more assimilable in the west, it will be through this sort of interpretation of cultural modes that we will come to discover what place it holds in our perspective of art, compared not only to other haiga, but to all other forms which we encounter.

In order to do this, we need to talk first a bit about haiku, as well as make a critical distinction in methods of viewing which is critical to the understanding of how haiga work.

Specifically, I would have you consider these two questions: "What are you looking at?" "What do you see?"

Looking is neutral, specific, representative. Looking is the act of an observer, and accepting of the reality observed. Looking makes sense and value based on the positing of an objective world "out there" and our ability to perceive it accurately. We act faithfully to that objective world, even if it is not certain that we are seeing it so. If I show you an image and ask you to identify it, and you can't, you might respond "I'm still looking." And your looking is taking place in the realm of the objective world where you might have seen such a sight before. (It's unlikely you'll say, in this activity, that it is the shape of a dream you had once, or of articles to be found on Mars—that would make them subjective or imaginative, or at least outside your experience, and wouldn't necessarily answer the question.)

Seeing, on the other hand, is an act of choice. It is the contemplation of not just things, but the relationship between things, and between things and ourselves. It is the act of an imaginer. Seeing is not satisfied solely with what is objectively noted, but seeks to make connections. It is intellective and categorical. It is associative, and "knows more" than the simple face of reality. It is subjective. Consider that image I asked you about a moment ago: if you didn't "understand" it at first, but came to do so, you might say "I see."

Looking is direct apprehension, and it requires an object; Looking says "I see *it*". Seeing is a step's remove, and requires no other object than the seer's mind and the connections found therein. Seeing says "I see".

There was a time when art was very simple. This does not mean art was not difficult to produce, or difficult to create. It means that its end result was not conceived to be outside of its own production. The artist created a symbol, and the symbol was usually as good a direct representation of the subject of his painting as he could make it. It was important to be good: successful art, successful magic, was thought to be the difference between feast times and famine, life and death, all and nothing.

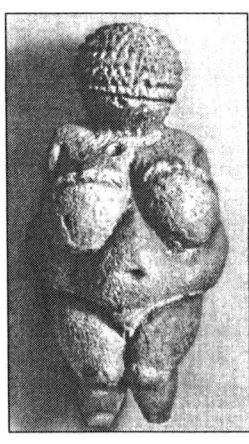

We have all been moved by the art of primitive peoples, such as the cave art as Lascaux and other places. We recognize it as art, not only because it is well formed, but because it shows selection, and art in the sense we generally employ the term suggests that some competence in using the tools of art is joined with some sense of vision, which is selection. Art in this sense commences when artists stop representing simply what they are looking at, and begin representing what they are seeing.

We, as people, are the direct heirs of this development. And as artists, we face this complexity and freedom even more than most people, since we know what it means to be faced with the empty canvas, the blank page. We know nothing is included except through our choices, and it is these choices—our taste, if you will—which is the single most important element of our art, more important that technique or message. Even when working in an established genre, nothing is a given—everything must be not only looked at, but chosen, created—seen.

All of which creates a paradox for us. One of the fundamental attitudes of haiku is the attainment of a selfless objectivity; that is, as pure a *looking* at things as we can manage. But surely it is impossible for us, as selves, ever to look at things as though we had no self. Even the negation of self comes from the self. Nevertheless, by accepting the conceit that it is possible to achieve such a "selfless" attitude—that is, by using creative vision, which is *seeing*, to advocate a particular technique, which we call *looking*—we find we can consider things in a new way. Blyth had it right when he said, "In haiku we attempt to *see* into the essence of things". (My emphasis.) Haiku, then, is a special kind of seeing, one which seemingly abnegates itself in favor of a

133

mythical looking as a desired quality in the manufacture of its final product. This fine and complex distinction is one of the great achievements of the mind.

This subtle interplay is more or less unstated in haiku and other similar verbal forms, but it becomes a good deal more obvious when the arena shifts to the visual. Almost without exception, the visual dominates the first impression of haiga. Because of the space, color and line of the visual element, it in nearly impossible for it to be otherwise. In the very few examples I have encountered where the ele-ments are more or less equal, it has come about by either enlarging the text to an abnormal degree, or else incorporating the text into the graphic plane in such a way that it is impossible not to read it integrally at the same time as taking in the illustration. These are serious technical considerations, and it is probably fair to say that the initial appeal of haiga must be visual. Besides these considerations, reaction to visual stimulus requires little or no articulation of the sort which is demanded by every text, regardless of its visual resources. Remember the Rothko, remember the Magritte. Feel the difference of demand each painting made upon you.

Consider, at the same time, that haiku is the most painterly of poetries, given as it is to images. Yet haiku are constructed, not of pictures, but of language. They perforce must utilize the artifices of language to communicate their images, their content. It is something of a miracle that language can be so seamless as to permit readers to enter an experience at such a distance from the actual event (or at least to permit us the fiction that they do). And this, of course, is what we, as poets who write haiku, are constantly seeking—a transparency of medium which does not distract by its presence from the greater purpose of the poem; or, as the famous anecdote has it, we strive to have noticed, not the pointing finger, but the moon.

Art, at least the art usually employed in haiga, likewise seeks to communicate seamlessly. But a picture, especially a simple and suggestive picture, though it may require the understanding of the syntax of space and line and color to understand how its effects are achieved, can have an immediate and non-mediated effect on the viewer. That is the goal of each piece of art, to create the world anew, containing its own way to value it.

Which brings us to the locus of difficulty in haiga: haiga is, by definition, a combinational art involving both pictorial and verbal elements. The level of complexity of such a representation jumps immeasurably. Though we may aim at simplicity, simplicity turns out to be a very complicated matter.

It is the control of complexity to achieve the simplicity of direct seeing which is the challenge of haiga. Its most common strategy is the visual equivalent of the functioning of haiku itself—it seeks a comparison between its image(s) and the image(s) of its attendent haiku. Which, too, is what the haiku is already attempting in its own right. And all this after an initial response to the visual material of the art itself. So what we have is an extremely complicated range of interplay. To keep these elements in balance and in such a way that each part is integral to the whole is no easy task. How can we accomplish it?

I believe the answer resides in what I will call the degree of closure available in the comparative elements. What this means is, how much the degree of complexity of the poem and illustration permit interaction, that is, how much looking versus how much seeing. The more objective, or realistic, or closed the image or poem, the less likely it will be able to interact sufficiently with its counterpart.

Consider, for instance, the haiga on the next page composed of a poem (written to the photo by Ernest J. Berry) and photograph (by Graeme Matthews). My feeling about this work, and the rest of the volume from which it was chosen (*a rainbow, a flowing river*), is that the poem feels tacked on here, more a caption than a co-equal partner in creation. Part of the reason for this is that the photograph is completely closed: it draws us powerfully to the "real" objective world, and away from our subjective

dead tree
alive with
life

world of imagination. The photograph, while it conjures things within us, does not require us to go beyond it for greater depth or interest. And so we stop there. The poem, coming after the fact of the impact of the visual element, has a great difficulty in holding its own. In fact, I don't think it's too much to say that haiga is anti-photography.

But it is not simply a matter, then, of creating openness. Too much openness defeats haiga in quite the opposite way: where there is not some part of seeing defined, then anything might be seen, that is, imagined, and such a work loses the inevitability which is the keen edge that whets us. Let's go back to the Rothko painting, for instance, and imagine it as part of a haiga. I have chosen several haiku by Tomizawa Kakio, as translated by Hiroaki Sato and appearing in the most recent *antantantantant*. I have not made any selections based on content here: I chose these poems because they were one-liners and therefore would fit under the painting well, and because the volume came easily to hand (it was on my desk). Consider, then, the combination Rothko/Tomizawa.

Autumn deep clanking our canteens we eat
Dead ahead clouds glittering forced to cross a river
There getting wet rain-red is a hand grenade
Night bandages with blood geese fly honking
The trench's belly blood-red undulating rains

Autumn deep clanking our canteens we eat. and *Dead ahead clouds glittering forced to cross a river.* and *There getting wet rain-red is a hand grenade.* and *Night bandage smudges with blood geese fly honking.* and *The trench's belly blood-red in undulating rains.* Certainly there was a bit of serendipity here, since the colors (in the original presentation, though not here in black and white) line up so nicely, and you might or might not like any or all of these, but even if you did, it would be hard to argue for any one more than any other beyond your liking. Each poem leads the viewer toward one of many arbitrary interpretations of the painting, none of which is necessarily any more valid than any other. This is merely the random juxtaposition of elements, made possible because the visual element is so open that it easily contains all these poems, and would contain millions more. The field here is one given completely to seeing, and it is inexhaustible, but this is not an argument for any one of the resulting combinations as a successful haiga.

This is a very fine thing to gauge, this degree of closure. And it is the central issue the creator of haiga must consider in order to succeed in his work. Almost certainly two sharply limned elements will fight one another, or at least invite the intellect to choose between them for superiority. This takes the viewer immediately out of the mindset necessary to enter the experience of the work. This is particularly true if it is the painting that is too accomplished, since it will dominate the initial response to the work.

Which is not to say that painters of haiga don't have to be highly skilled: they must be good enough to accomplish without overstating, and to judge the sort of interaction their image will have with the text. They must be good enough to realize the effect their work will have on the viewer, and then be accomplished enough not to overwhelm, or especially, close the imagination. And they must still create work of visual interest.

The most succesful haiga, then, are those pieces which can manage this.

Let's consider, then, the strategies which creators of haiga generally employ. If, as we have said, the visual element predominates during the first glance, then there are basically two tactics available to the artist: the first is representational, and the second is non-representational. In the first, the visual element is easily understood at a glance or at least with some minimal attention. It needs to be attractive enough to induce the viewer into looking at the poem, but not so finished as to end the discussion all by itself. In the second, the visual element is not clear, and the array of picture and poem suggests, in most instances, that the text might be consulted to clarify. Still, it must be of sufficient interest that the poem not seem informational or a caption.

Our first example is by perhaps the greatest master of the form. Buson was an extremely accomplished artist. He was more than capable of creating visual art that was entirely self-sufficient in capturing the attention of an audience. But he was also a great haijin, and in his interest in developing both arts, he was able to adjust the balance of the two as no other artist before or since. This example is somewhat typical of his work, neither his best nor worst attempts. It is instructive to see how he manages to make this slight poem, and this sketchy drawing, work together as a cohesive whole. The poem—*young bamboo / and Hashimoto courtesans, / are they here too?*—is really little more than a conventional metaphor. And the drawing, again a somewhat stylized rendition of a traditional theme, the sprouting bamboo of spring, is no great effort considered against his entire oeuvre. But the glue which binds these two

conventional elements and pieces together is his barely suggested hut, a few sketchy lines which seem almost hidden even in this sparse growth. The bamboo, the hut, the direct metaphor of the poem, can all be seen as representational. No effort is made to suggest anything but the direct experience. And yet, as Buson represents it, there is a reticence and mystery which arises, and more to these conventions that meets the eye. What it is is hidden from us, hidden by the very convention itself, which the artist suggests in a most delicate way.

The second, the non-representational strategy, walks the tricky ground that we encountered when we played with the Rothko painting. It needs to be visually interesting, but not closed. And it needs to be sufficiently closed so as not to admit unlimited numbers of poems to accompany. Look at this unusual painting, and try not to read the poem before figuring out what the image is. Even after reading the poem—*no color or scent / when flower viewing— / stuffy nose*—it's not absolutely certain what we're looking at. Is it a nose? If it is, I would agree it's a stuffy one. But it might be something else, and the title, *Self Portrait*, would tend to make us think it might be something more than just a nose. It is the non-representational aspect of this image that pulls us in, and makes us seek out the poem. At the same time, there is nothing else in the painting other than the poem and the poet's signature, so it certainly is not closed: we can imagine all sorts of things, we can enjoy the humor of the poet's predicament, and we are left with a bit of a puzzle and a suffiently open juxtaposition to allow us to feel both a participant and an observer. Looking and seeing.

This is the critical element in how haiga work. It is not enough to have technical skill in either or both of these art forms, it is also important that the artist be able to manage them both to permit the audience a way to participate in the work, and at the same time limit the number of possible satisfactory juxtapositions. We've already seen two very different strategies to accomplish this, and both of these strategies employ their own tactics to achieve their aims.

There are three basic models which the creator of haiga has at his disposal. Each of which has its merits and its difficulties, its usefulness of application as well as drawbacks. These tactics are used in both classical and contemporary work, so it will be interesting to compare them down through the ages.

The first model is that of the poem/portrait. Here the  painter, who in classical treatment is sometimes the poet as well but most usually not, offers homage to a poet by presenting one of his verses accompanied by a portrait. This is a powerful political commentary, because such an arrangement can have the effect of legitimizing the poem, the poet, and the artist all at the same time. In this famous example, Buson has painted Basho's portrait, and appends the following poem: *mono ieba / kuchibiru samushi / aki-no kaze. when speaking / the lips turn cold—/ autumn wind*. This is not a casual sketch, jotted quickly. This is from the tradition of high art, with calculated effects and sure technique. It functions in the way that mainstream art usually functions, by appropriating the symbols of power recognized in the technique and exploiting them.

This is certainly not one of the most famous or revered

poems by Basho, but is greatly enhanced by this cleverly planned and powerfully rendered portrait. Basho appears far older here than in any other portraits from any period in his life (and we need to remember that he died at age fifty-one), with the apparent strategy to align with convention of portraying wisdom through agedness. Buson is claiming a spiritual kinship with Basho, and honoring him by painting him wiser, that is, older, than he in fact was. Notice too how the figure of Basho, though dead now for over a hundred years, flows out to more than fill the space. His presence remains overwhelming to the painter even after all these years. The traveling clothes also suggest Basho's common humanity. And, as the self-proclaimed direct descendant, spiritually, of Basho, Buson claims all these powers for himself as well.

Basho is easily the most popular subject for such haiga. And this is instructive, too, not merely because it tells us that many other Japanese (and other) artists wish to create an alliance with the grand old man of Japanese poetry, but because it also tells us so much about the manner in which haiga is created. It might be argued that portraiture is closed, that it tries to create a fully self-sufficient world around its subject. And yet the variety of portraits of Basho is the most cogent argument against this. He is portrayed as young, old, jolly, stern, well and ill, deep in thought and utterly vapid. Even though it might be argued that portrait haiga is simply a subset of representational haiga, it has been so commonly practiced, and with such variety, it deserves its own place in the history of the form.

Not all portraits are so grand, as we have seen in Shiro's work, and the next, by Issa. The poem attached is: *even considered / in the most favourable light, / he looks cold.* The sidelong glance which Issa shares with the viewer suggests a puckish humor, as though the inconvenience of cold is not taken very seriously, though at least worthy of his notice, and this casual sketch. In reality, though, this is anything but a casual piece: Issa rewrote this poem at least six times with varying emphases, and also sketched himself

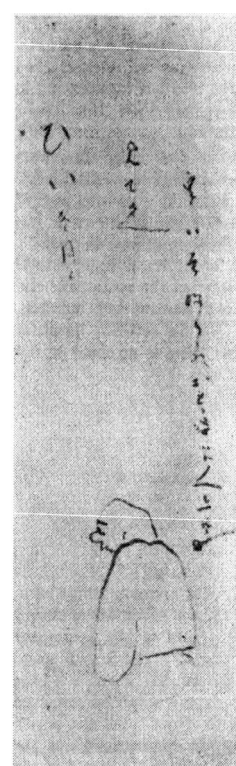

in this similar pose at least one other time, not to mention the preliminary sketches he might have tried and discarded. Achieving simplicity is no easy feat.

Issa's methodology is instructively different from Buson's. He was in no way a comparable artist, and is wise not to elaborate his sketches. What he achieves, similar to his written work, is a disarming vulnerability, a kind of naïf art where clumsiness is a precondition to eloquence. As the haiga painter Watanabe Kazan states in his *Absorption in Pleasure*: "With morning glories, the clumsier you paint them, the more pathos they have." This point of view is critically central to what is most effective in haiga, and Issa is one of the best exemplars of such an aesthetic.

The second model we might call iterative haiga. By this I mean haiga in which the subject matter of the picture and the poem are identical, and are intended to reinforce each other. Again, this is not so simple as it might seem. If either of the elements overpowers, it will render the other extraneous. In fact, this is the most common mistake we encounter in contemporary haiga, especially in the west. But when done well, there is a building of

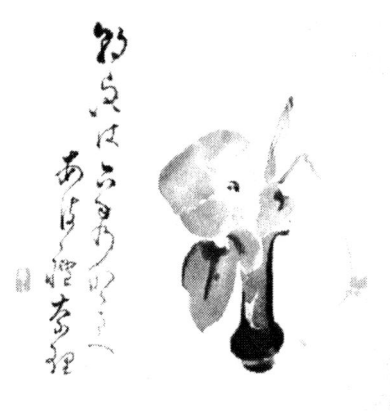

power, a heightened exerience of the central image. Consider, for instance, the aforementioned Watanabe's *morning glories*. The poem can be considered a mere apothegm, or worse, an excuse for a poorly executed painting. But instead, because the painting so charmingly illustrates the point, the art and text reinforce each other, and we are glad for both.

Another example of this is Hakuin's *wren*. The poet

makes fun of his own inability to paint to a sufficient standard, but in so doing makes a virtue of it. (The poem: *It looks like a nightingale, but it's a wren!*) The painting here can be considered artless, but there is still a liveliness which the poem points to obliquely, even while simply recounting what the painting is about.

Both of these haiga, and others equally successful, work because the predisposition we have towards them from the visual is not overwhelming. They are artless, charming, inviting. We are enticed into considering the poem as well, because we know the painting has not said all there is to say of the situation. And once we encounter the poem, we are directed back to the painting through the repetition of theme. These modest paintings carry, as a result, a bit more energy than they might on their own. Likewise, the poems are saved from preciousness by their associations with art which redeems them. Looking at these haiga does not preclude a further seeing into them.

Both of these examples are representational. We might recall Shiro's self-portrait as an example of a non-representational picture paired with a thematically linked poem—that is, if we agree it is not a picture of a nose, but of something abstracted.

The final model is tangential haiga, where the art and the poem do not share a theme explicitly, but speak to one another in a glancing fashion, the one opening the other. These are often the most resonant haiga, since the worlds contained in the two elements, not necessarily conjoined in our minds prior to the haiga, are brought together when the two images comment upon one another. Here is Soken's *full moon*.

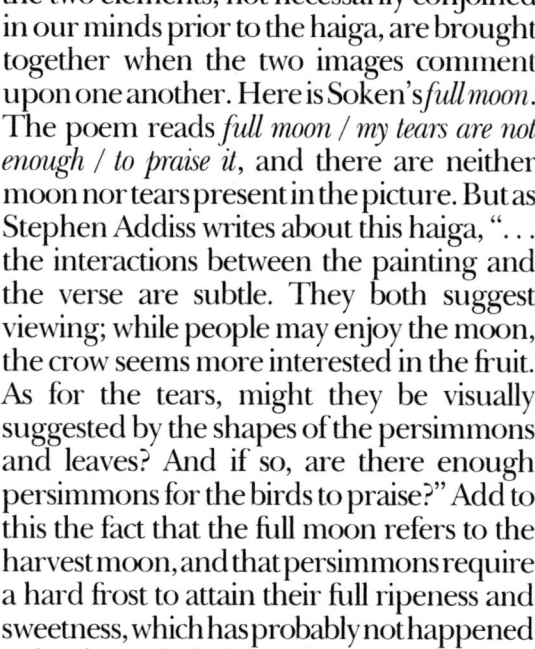

The poem reads *full moon / my tears are not enough / to praise it*, and there are neither moon nor tears present in the picture. But as Stephen Addiss writes about this haiga, "... the interactions between the painting and the verse are subtle. They both suggest viewing; while people may enjoy the moon, the crow seems more interested in the fruit. As for the tears, might they be visually suggested by the shapes of the persimmons and leaves? And if so, are there enough persimmons for the birds to praise?" Add to this the fact that the full moon refers to the harvest moon, and that persimmons require a hard frost to attain their full ripeness and sweetness, which has probably not happened yet—it's too early—but which should be occurring soon. The objects of the crow's desire is not ready for consuming, and that's reason enough for tears; but once ripe, surely tears will not be praise enough.

Another excellent example of this threaded sort of

connection is Ryota's *charcoal basket*. The poem reads *looking at the light / there is a wind / this night of snow*. But the picture shows none of the image presented in the poem, but rather the charcoal basket, which allows the whole to take on a cozier aspect, a mingling of warmth with the chill. What is more beautiful than watching the freeflight of descending snowflakes when we are comfortably warm? The charcoal basket is casually sketched, and as though aware of its peripheral status in the poem actually falls off the edge of the paper. The hint of wind is caught in the calligraphy, with its sinuous curves and wide vertical spacings. The visual is definitely subordinated to the verbal in this work, but in such a beguiling fashion, and so modestly, that it is easily assimilated into the cosmos limned by the poem, and in fact infinitely deepens it.

Again these are representational examples, but non-representational ones abound. Consider another work by the inimitable Shiro, *moon*. The moon is nowhere to be found, and the visual element is reduced to a single line to represent the mountain who is the genius of the poem. Does the moon illumine the bare outline of this mountain? Or are we waiting for this moon to rise above it, or sink beneath it? It is impossible to say. Much is suggested by this extreme minimalist offering, and the poem is much the better for its accompaniment.

These, then, are the six categories of haiga which have held the interest of poets and painters through the tradition to the present day. Other traditions, such as the animistic painting of creatures acting as humans, widely practiced five hundred years ago, has died out as faith in a literal interpretation in animism has been superseded by more contemporary creeds. The six are, again: representational portrait haiga; non-representational portrait haiga; representational iterative haiga; non-representational iterative haiga; representational tangential haiga; non-representational tangential haiga.

Each of these categories are still utilized today, but as you might expect, each has been updated to include more modern subject matter, tools and techniques. It is not uncommon to find haiga created on the computer, or incorporating unusual materials in the painting, or including modern content in the poems. All these things are essential if haiga is to be a modern form, if it is to be an available form for poets and painters to express their contemporary condition aesthetically. Similarly, the aesthetic which has been identified with haiga, as with haiku, is shifting as painters and poets from more cultures turn their attention to these forms. It is a sign of vitality that the form seems to be able to accomodate these changes without losing its overall shape, and I anticipate that haiga will continue to grow as its best work is exposed to a larger audience in more and different places around the globe.

I would like to close with some examples of each of the six categories by artists from some of these various cultures. First, a quartet of portrait haiga, ranging from representational to non-representational.

The most traditional of these is this portrait of Santoka by the Japanese graphic artist Kuniharu Shimizu. What makes this interesting is the way in which the artist combines the old portrait tradition.

One remove from this is my own piece, *after midnight*. The poem goes: *after midnight / the oddness of / my self*. I think one of the most important aspects of this work, in terms of keeping the graphic open and inviting to the viewer to consider the poem as well, is the way the eyes are closed. This creates a suggestion of interiority, which corresponds with the poem's sense of individual quirkiness as well. The likeness is no worse a likeness, I suppose, than Shiro's nose.

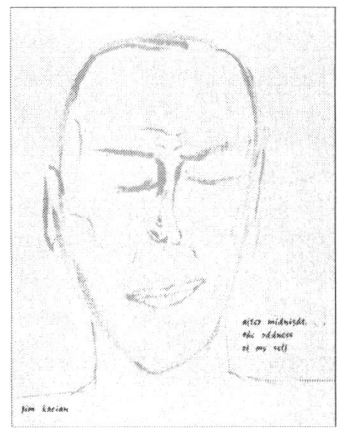

Occupying a sort of middle ground in these is David Gershator's computer-generated portrait. The artist doesn't indicate who the picture is intended to be: is it the artist himself? Is it yet another image of Basho? Is it some other person, a cyberperson, perhaps, trapped in the

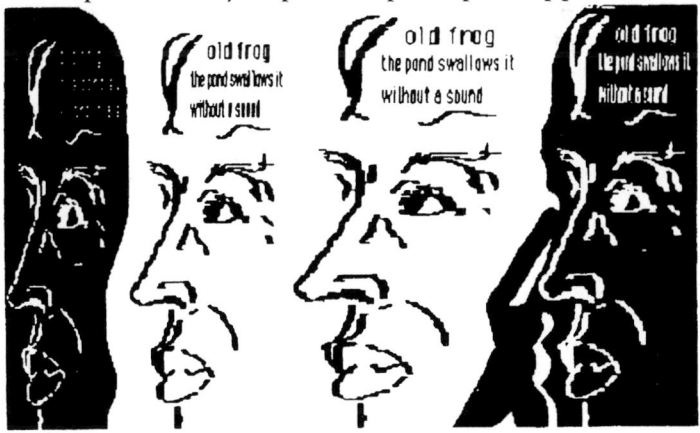

resonance of the old pond reverberating electrons for yet another generation of haiku poets? There are interesting questions about this work which I don't think can be answered entirely to our satisfaction. And with its now old-fashioned bit-mapped computer graphics, we experience a kind of post-modern *wabi* where none could have expected it. A most complex piece of art.

The last of this group is even further removed. The subject of the portrait is Jackson Pollock, and the poem reads: *mad flicker in eye / pollocks bearish figure plods / rain awakens night.* I confess to liking this work more and more as time goes by. The artist, Guy Beining, does not appropriate Pollock's style for the portrait, but something chunkier and more object-oriented. It most reminds me of the drawings of Bob Dylan, with its similar unlikeliness of line and oddities of objects and their relationships. And what might have simply been fortuitous, the marker with which Beining adds the poem seems to have been drying up, causing an interesting attenuation of the poem, just as the rain awakens the night. A very modern sort of portrait.

We can run the gamut between representational and non-representational iterative haiga as well. Consider, at the front end of that spectrum, Jeanne Emrich's work entitled *winter moon*. If the poem was calligraphed in Japanese instead of English we would have no difficulty believing this was a work from the Edo period. It has a

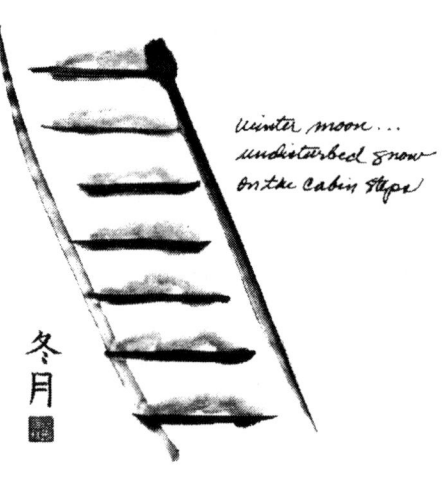

beautiful control of the image, suggestive but not overblown, and it links directly with the poem: *winter moon . . . / undisturbed snow / on the cabin steps*. A slight flaw is that both painting and poem draw on the same store of images, and so the one isn't appreciably enlarged by the other.

A bit less direct a connection is made in Borivoj Bukva's haiga *daljine me zovu*. The figures in the picture, wanderers of the sort we imagine Basho to have been, or more recently, Santoka, might be found as well in Bukva's native Croatia, though probably without this sort of hat. The text of the poem translates to: *distance calls me / and I'll disappear / into it*. The use of watercolor, especially to blur the images, is effective in this work, an echo of the same fading before the vanishing point which the poem suggests. The looking does not eliminate the seeing here either: the two figures are engaged in some sort of communication, a moment's pleasantness along the way, but the poem communicates a much more solitary position, where such human contact seems far removed, a luxury we rarely have.

stepping, painting by Susan Frame, poem by Jeanne Emrich, approaches non-representational iterative haiga.

Only small portions of the art are recognizably representational, a hint, if you will, but it is enough to ground the picture. What to make of the blotches and blurs of the rest of the painting is left for the poem to explicate: *stepping / into the woods / the moon follows*. The moon seems missing from this painting: perhaps the roundness of the shapes Frame finds in the woods is sufficiently suggestive.

It is truly difficult to find a totally non-representative iterative haiga. Almost by definition, if the painting and the poem are going to treat the same subject, the painting must be sufficiently representative that we can know that it is the same theme. A painting that was completely beyond interpretation in some literal sense would also play randomly against any poem paired with it, and so it is unlikely any poem would seem inevitable in such combination. However, it is possible to move pretty far afield toward this unreachable endpoint. Two strategies seem particularly rewarding. Both rely upon suggestibility for their effect.

The first is abstract expressionism. In this haiga, art by Wilfred Croteau, poem by Raffael de Gruttola, the painting

considered by itself seems to be primarily about painting, that is, about lines and planes and masses. But in the context of the poem, which reads *frozen pond / an oak leaf / half in / half out*, we see that the one has a substantial intersection of content with the other. Which is not to say that this bold line breaking the plane is a leaf out of ice. But it is useful to know that the art was produced in response to the poem, and so certainly informed the sorts of choices the artist might make in creating a finished product.

The second strategy is abstract realism. If we just consider the graphic element in this haiga, one of my own, before you know it is called *sun-warmed sea*, it might suggest any number of possible interpretations. But paired with the poem, which reads the sun-warmed sea not knowing where I leave off, we are placed specifically. And yet not so specifically, since the poem articulates an interior state of identification. The graphic might just as easily be a pictorial version of this unification, a sort of topography of identification. The original gradient scale of colors moves from a warm and fecund sea green to a royal and mystical deep blue, providing emotional latitude for interpretation.

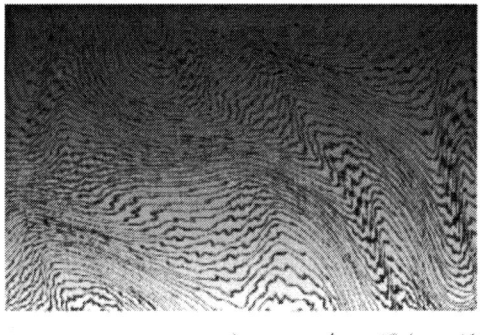

the sun-warmed sea not knowing where I leave off

Finally, let's consider the range of modern possibilities for tangential haiga. By definition we should not expect the art to repeat the theme of the poem; however, we should expect there to be some sort of linkage between the images of the one and the other. Otherwise we would be back to the random pairing of images, and the looking would not lend itself to an inevitable and resonant seeing.

I start with Stephen Addiss's simple and evocative *broom*. This, too, could easily have come from an earlier time. The poem, *motes of dust / sparkling / in November sunlight*, is a simple appreciation of the joys of ordinary life, rather reminiscent of the poems of Ryokan. The painting is an unadorned broom. The technique is familiar to us. The pairing is felicitous: I suppose it is possible to say it is a sort of cause-and-effect. And this is nicely gauged, since we experience the broom first, and the poem second: it feels right to come to discover the sunlit motes after having enjoyed the perkily-sketched broom.

motes of dust
sparkling

in November sunlight

AS

The airiness we feel from this work is one of its chief characteristics, befitting a celebration of flying dust motes.

Contrast that with the weight of this next work, *sesame oil* by Arizona Zipper. Working with pencil and magic marker, the artist fills up the available space, and we feel a snugness,

which is not oppressive, partly because we can view the lines of the drawing beneath the fill, which have not been adhered to in a very strict fashion. The image, a bird at the birdbath, is refreshing itself. In just the same way, sipping a cool draught from an unexpected source while flying by, the poet has enjoyed a moment of humor in the midst of his life: *my friend from the city pleased that I've sesame oil in the larder*. The slight smile from the oddity of another's expectation is the contrasting lightness to the heaviness of the painting, and paralleled neatly in the lightness of the bird.

Almost to the brink of non-representational tangential haiga is Angelee Deodhar's painting, to one of my poems, *rumble*. It could be argued that the painter actually visualizes a completely different scene, but one which is contiguous to, or even contained in, the poem. The poem goes: *snow falling everywhere / the rumble of a jet / goes on and on*. You might expect snow falling in a picture of this poem, but the artist here actually dispenses with it, and instead posits a moon to permit us to see into the depths of a perilous ravine. It is the present

snow falling everywhere
the rumble of a jet
goes on and on

snow which permits us to see how steep and precarious it is. And the rumble? Surely a rumble in such country would mean avalanche. So the one conjures the other, and perhaps might even precipitate it. Quite a nice redefining of the locus of the center of attention, with a consequent enlargement of the possibilities of both images.

At last we reach total non-representationality with this final haiga, Zolo's *something I'll never find*. The image is a blur of activity, with some strong features emerging from

the first snowfall . . .
searching for something I know
I'll never find

out of the maelstrom. It is impossible to be certain where we are, but the image suggests nothing to me so much as hairs on the skin, and our vantage point then some extreme close-up of a living body. The poem disabuses us of this idea—but only for a moment. It reads: *the first snowfall . . . / searching for something I know / I'll never find*. So we could be in the woods, but more likely we are in the interior spaces of the artist's mind, and this is some figurative version of hell, a hell where the only certainty is that of frustration.

That completes our tour of contemporary haiga. As you can see, there is no shortage of possibility in the field, and artists of widely divergent talent, style and intention are exploring it. Perhaps you will be inspired to explore it yourselves. And as you do so, perhaps you will consider not only how your pictures look, but how they are seen.

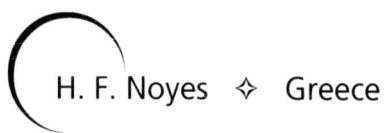

H. F. Noyes ✧ Greece

A Favorite Haiku

eyes closed
knowing by heart
the rest[1]
Jane Reichhold

As an illustration of how divergent interpretations of haiku can be, at the risk of committing sacrilege—but with Jane's permission—I have chosen her beautiful and fervent memorial to Raymond Roseliep. It is a full-hearted testament to intimacy of the closest kind. Is it any wonder that I make the association with love-making? With a lover we pass from treating one anonther as virtual objects, in the sensuality of foreplay, to what the heart most desires—surrender of self in the deep sense of oneness. The tension of separate individuality is released in the "oceanic" feeling that brings a unique sense of peace. The final word "rest" comes as a stroke of genius in this haiku, whether we think of the serenity of "interbeing" or of "the last sleep."

---

1. *Brussels Sprout* XI:1

Two Favorite Haiku

A chestnut falls.
The insects cease their crying
Among the grasses.[1]

April snowflakes—
Just enough to bend
The daffodil leaves.[2]

Though an element of *yugen* mystery is much more likely in haiku of interpenetration or "dependent co-arising", an interdiction against cause-and-effect in haiku would be absurd, as it is a major aspect of the lifeflow. Dozens upon dozens of the best haiku of the old masters are cause-and-effect. Of the two Basho haiku above, it is the clearly cause-and-effect example that I find most likable, most natural and spontaneous—a delicate example of *karumi* lightness. The first is a fine representative of the Jungian synchronicity theory that simultaneous occurrences are interrelated, and of the wonder element in haiku.

---
1. *Parabola* magazine, Spring 1997: Richard Lewis, "Living by Wonder"
2. R. H. Blyth, *Haiku, Vol. I*

Make It Happen

Sometimes a haiku arouses thoughts that seem well worth sharing. An instance is this one by Geraldine C. Little:

> how silently
> the wave-tossed log is beached
> and snow-flaked[1]

The phrase, "Make it happen," which editors occasionally use when our haiku don't quite "hit home", merits contemplation. What is this? Doesn't it have to do with igniting the spark of spirit? I'm so partial, myself, to the earthy "suchness" of Zen that I used to feel uncomfortable with Blyth's assertion that Basho's aspiration was to see through the eyes of God. And I remember being embarrassed by the poet Stephen Spender's description of a gull in flight as "writing memoirs of God".

Now I dare to ask whether this isn't what *we* are sometimes doing in a fine haiku—even one as simple as Shiki's about birdsong "knocking down" a berry. In the haiku cited above, though each word is essential, the deepest *sabi* truth is—as always—in the wordless resonance. Its inner voices speak to us in "the silent allusion of things" to something "now and forever," common to every great religion. It evokes some ineffable universal essence that is Reality in the eye of God.

In a pack of French tarot cards I came across the expression, "Par lui le monde s'eveille": roughly "through it the world awakens." Here again we have that elusive spark. Isn't it something of the spirit which is generated through our true living of any eternal moment—a moment that weds present-mindedness with the infinite? Now that modern physics clearly confirms the working partnership between nature and spirit, it is easier to believe that we haikuists have a role, however humble—however "down to earth" our language—through the transmission of our authentic haiku moments, in awakening the world to the mystery and miracle of everyday "ordinary" life.

> no one to see
> the wind filling out
> the faraway flags

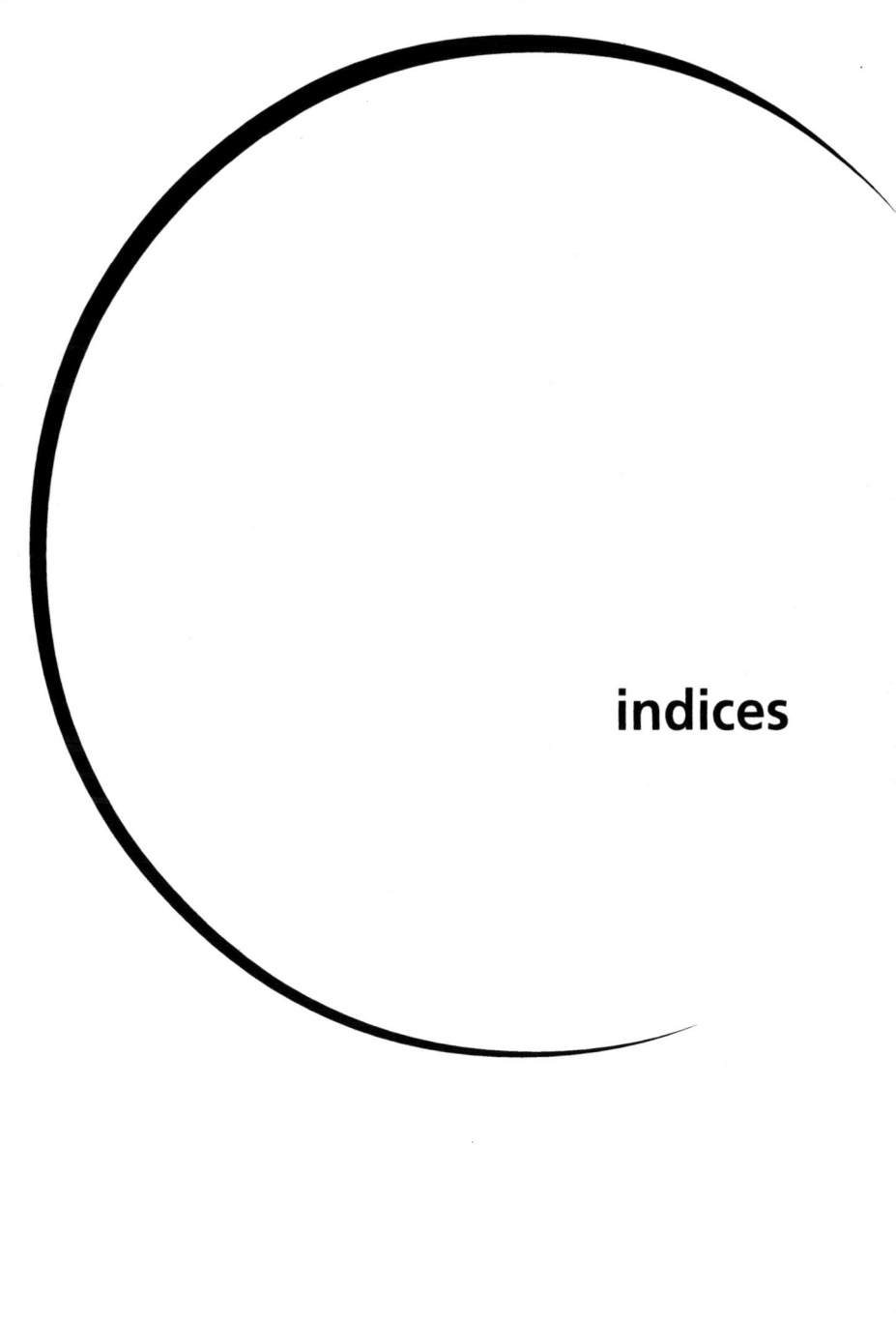
indices

index of authors

Addiss, Stephen...9
Amor, Stephen...9
angela, frances...10
Aoyagi, Fay...11

Baker, Deb...85
Baker, Winona...11
Barry, Jack...12
Beaven, Louise...12
Berry, Ernest J...13
Bird, John...14
Blaine, Michael...14
Buettner, Marjorie...15
Butterworth, Sheila...15

Cabalona, Yvonne...16, 56
Carter, R. P...16
Chang, Yu...17
Chula, Margaret...18
Clausen, Tom...19
Close, Charles...19
Cobb, David...87-88
Cobb, Kathy Lippard...20
Cudney, Katherine...21, 89-91
Cullen, William Jr...22

Dahl, DeVar...23
Davidson, Anne LB...23
Daw, Ian...24
Day, Cherie Hunter...24
Deming, Kristen...25
Deodhar, Angelee...25
Dillon, Mike...26
Dixon, Melissa...92-94
Donleycott, Connie...27
Dorsty, George...26
Dudley, Michael...28

Elliott, David...95-96

Emrich, Jeanne...28, 97
Engle, Margaret...98
Epstein, Robert...29
Estevez, Efrem...117-120
Evetts, Dee...121-125

Fowler, James...99-100

Gage, Joshua...29
Gallagher, D. Claire...30
Gay, Garry...30
George, Barry...31
George, Beverley...31
Gierat, Brian...32
Gilbert, Joyce Austin...32
Gilli, Ferris...33
Gilliland, Robert...34
Gorman, LeRoy...34
Gourlay, Caroline...35
Grimnes, Kay...35
Gurga, Lee...36

Hall, Carolyn...36, 109, 110
Hawkes, Timothy...37
Heinrich, Peggy...37
Herold, Christopher...38
Higginson, William...111
Holzer, Ruth...39
Hooper, Olga...39
Hotham, Gary...40
Houlder, Vicky...40

James, Kevin...41
Jamieson, Tim...41
Jones, Ken...42

Kacian, Jim...43, 101, 126-153
Kilbride, Jerry...42
King, Nancy Tripp...102

Klein, Karen...44
Klontz, Joann...44
Kolodji, Deborah P...45
Kunova, Ekaterina...45

Lamb, Charles...46
Lather, Rajiv...103-104
Leuck, Angela...105
Lippy, Burnell...46
Lucas, Martin...47
Lyles, Peggy Willis...47

m., paul...48
Markowski, Ed...49
Martin, Jeanne...49
McAdoo, Brynne...106-107
McClintock, Michael...50
McCullough, Dan...50
McGill, Allen...51
McLaughlin, Dorothy...51
McLeod, Adelaide...52
Meyerhofer, Michael...52
Missias, A. C...53
Miyashita, Emiko...53
Moore, Lenard D...54
Morden, Matt...54
Mountain, Marlene...55

Ness, Pamela Miller...56
Noyes, H. F...154-156

Ortiz, Victor...55
owen, w. f...57

Painting, Tom...58
Patchel, Christopher...60
Pfleuger, Paul Jr...59
Pizzarelli, Alan...60
Porad, Francine...61
Proctor, Vanessa...61

Reeves, Lyn...62
Ristic, Dragan...62
Robinson, Chad Lee...63
Romano, Emily...64
Russell, Timothy...64

Sagan, Miriam...65
Scott, Rob...66
Shaw, Adelaide B...65
Shimi...67
Shimizu, Kuniharu...67
Sohne, Karen...68
Spence, Alan...69
Stanford, Sue...68
Stevenson, John...70
Sterba, Carmen...72
Sternlieb, Barry...108
Stoelting, Laurie, W...71
Story, Ebba...109
Swede, George...72

Tann, Hilary...73
Tarquinio, Rick...74
Tasker, Brian...112
Tasnier, Maurice...74
Tauchner, Dieter...75
Tico, Tom...75
tripi, vincent...78
Trumbull, Charles...76

Walker, Marilyn Appl...78
Walsh, Frank...79
Welch, Michael Dylan...77, 112, 113
Wilson, Billie...112

Yarrow, Ruth...79
Yoshimura, Ikuyo...113
Young, Nancy S...80
Yovu, Peter...80

Zackowitz, Cindy...81
Zambito, Matt...81

acknowledgments

Addiss—"reappearing" *South by Southeast* XI:1; **Amor**—"a field of crickets" *The Heron's Nest* 6:2; **angela**—"garden party" *Mayfly* 37, "backwards" *Presence* 22; **Aoyagi**—"a hole in my sweater" *Mariposa* 11; **Baker, D.**—"The Embroidered Quilt" *contemporary haibun* 5; **Baker, W.**—"office party" *Modern Haiku* 34:1; **Barry**—"a beaver's wake" *acorn* 12; **Beavan**—"back at" Kaji Aso Contest 2004; **Berry**—"long eulogy" *Presence* 24, "2nd honeymoon" *Yellow Moon* 15, "first light" *Mariposa* 10; **Bird**—"winter sun" *Shadow Poetry Quill* 2004 Volume 2; **Blaine**—"moving day" *Frogpond* XXVII:1; **Buettner**—"a deep roundness" *bottle rockets* 10; **Butterworth**—"midmorning bus" *Presence* 22; **Cabalona**—"dragonfly" and "My Father's Daughter" *Mariposa* 11; **Carter**—"around" *Frogpond* XXVII:3; **Chang**—"birdsong" *The Heron's Nest* VI:2, "xxx" *Frogpond* XXVII:3; **Chula**—"end of summer" "carrying moonlight" "war begins" *The Smell of Rust*; **Clausen**—"left and right" *Frogpond* XXVII:2; **Close**—"reunion photo" *The Heron's Nest* VI:7; **Cobb, D.**—"A Hole with a View" "The Priest Hole of Oxburgh Hall" *Forefathers*; **Cobb, K.**—"missing child" *Presence* 24, "afternoon calm" *Shiki Internet Salon*; **Cudney**—"a heart-shaped pebble" "a purple tree" *The Heron's Nest* VI:7, "Untied" *Modern Haiku* 35:1; **Cullen**—"Earth Day" *Modern Haiku* 35:1, "sand storm" *acorn* 12; **Dahl**—"first day at school" *Presence* 22; **Davidson**—"beside the road" *Haiku Canada Newsletter* XVII:1; **Daw**—"holding" *Presence* 22; **Day**—"hopscotch grid" *The Heron's Nest* VI:5; **Deming**—"drifting snow" *Modern Haiku* 35:3; **Deodhar**—"a child's haiku" *bottle rockets* 10; **Dillon**—"the distance between" *acorn* 12; **Dixon**—"The Conspiracy" *contemporary haibun* 5; **Donleycott**—"summer garden" "creak of the swing" *The Heron's Nest* VI:2; **Dorsty**—"dead hamster" *The Heron's Nest* VI:7; **Dudley**—"deep winter" *Frogpond* XXVII:1; **Elliott**—"Independence Day" *RAW NerVZ* IX:4; **Emrich**—"Pleiades at dawn" *The Heron's Nest* VI:7, "Breath" *contemporary haibun* 5; **Engle**—"Elementary Hindi-Urdu" *contemporary haibun* 5; **Epstein**—"open window" *Modern Haiku* 35:3; **Estevez**—"Images of John Wills" *Frogpond* XXVII:1; **Evetts**—"The Conscious Eye: Urban Haiku" *Frogpond* XXVII:2; **Fowler**—"War" *contemporary haibun* 5; **Gage**—"call from the hospital" *The Heron's Nest* VI:2; **Gallagher**—"breakwater" *Frogpond* XXVII:2; **Gay**—"River stones" *Mariposa* 11; **George, Ba.**—"heat lightning" *paper wasp* Spring 2004; **George, Be.**—"lengthening shadow" BHS James W Hackett International Haiku Award 2003; **Gierat**—"the corner" *Heron's Nest* VI:2; **Gilbert**—"after his death" Kaji Aso Contest 2004; **Gilli**—"lakeside memorial" *Frogpond* XXVII:2, "hallowed ground" *acorn* 12; **Gilliland**—"Valentine's Day" *The Heron's Nest* VI:3; **Gorman**—"cattle sold" *bottle rockets* 12; **Gourlay**—"eating in silence" *Modern Haiku* 35:2; **Grimnes**—"cicadas" *The Heron's Nest* V:12; **Gurga**—"midday heat" *Modern Haiku* 35:1; **Hall**—"slave cemetery" *The Heron's Nest* VI:2, "Clack of the Rails", "Lingering Light" *Mariposa* 10; **Hawkes**—"faint stars" *The Heron's Nest* VI:2; **Heinrich**—"half-empty bed" *The Heron's Nest* VI:9; **Herold**—"hothouse tour" *Modern Haiku* 35:3, "more deaths in Iraq" *Hermitage* 1 & 2, "autumn sunset" HPNC Contest 2004; **Higginson**—"The Small Hours" *Modern Haiku* 35:3; **Holzer**—"gathering shells" *bottle rockets* 10; **Hooper**—"Monkey Year" Kaji Aso Contest 2004; **Hotham**—"the nail sinking in" *The Heron's Nest* VI:21; **Houlder**—"bright moon" *Blithe Spirit* XIV:2; **James**—"late supper" *acorn* 12; **Jamieson**—"a ripple in the lake" *Haiku Canada Newsletter* XVI:4; **Jones**—"heavy evening" *Blithe Spirit* 14:1; **Kacian**—"first warm day" *acorn* 12, "telling stories" *Mariposa* 11, "lightning" *Ten* 115, "one main street" *Mariposa* 10, "by the Flat River" *Mariposa* 11, "mutatis" *contemporary haibun* 5, "Looking and Seeing" *Simply Haiku*; **Kilbride**—"year of the monkey" *Mariposa* 11; **King**—"Washday" *contemporary haibun* 5; **Klein**—"cold snap" Kaji Aso Contest 2004; **Klontz**—"my lapsed religion" *Frogpond* XXVII:2; **Kolodji**—"Christmas light test" *bottle rockets* 10; **Kunova**—"the bus station" *The Road*; **Lamb**—"nagasaki" 38th A-Bomb Memorial Day Contest; **Lather**—"The Wait" *Frogpond* XXVII:1; **Leuck**—"Winter Morning" *Haiku Canada Newsletter* XVII:2; **Lippy**—"winter plant" *The Heron's Nest* VI:9; **Lucas**—"a cloud of gnats" *Blithe Spirit* 14:3; **Lyles**—"the scent" *acorn* 12; **m.**—"rain today" *The Heron's Nest* VI:8, "dusk" *Ko Autumn/Winter* 2004, "Mother's Day" *Modern Haiku* 35:3; **Markowski**—"december lay off" *RAW NerVZ* IX:4; **Martin**—"dry riverbed" *hummingbird* XIV:2; **McAdoo**—"Haiku Rendezvous" *Frogpond* XXVII:2; **McClintock**—"a puppet taken" *The Heron's Nest* VI:2; **McCullough**—"releasing" *acorn* 13; **McGill**—"storm clouds" *The Heron's Nest* VI:2; **McLaughlin**—"morning commute" *bottle rockets* 10; **McLeod**—"the last words" *Frogpond* XXVII:3; **Meyerhofer**—"mentioning divorce" *acorn* 12; **Missias**—"spring sun" *dim sum* 2004/1; **Miyashita**—"early spring" *Hermitage* 1 & 2; **Moore**—"hot afternoon" *The Heron's Nest* VI:9; **Morden**—"higher and higher" *Haiku Canada Newsletter* XVII:1; **Mountain**—"the moon" *Frogpond* XXVII:3; **Ness**—"autumn equinox" *Haiku Canada Newsletter* XVII:3, "talk of divorce" *acorn* 13, "birthday morning" *Frogpond* XXVII:3; **Noyes**—"A Favorite Haiku" *xxx*, "Two Favorite Haiku" *xxx*, "Making It Happen" *xxx*; **Ortiz**—"suture scars" *Frogpond* XXVII:2; **owen**—"longest day" *Acorn* 12, "summer dusk" *Mariposa* 10, "rain all day" *Frogpond* XXVII:1; **Painting**—"paint by number" *bottle rockets* 10, "animal skull" *The Heron's Nest* VI:2, "peace rally" 38th A-Bomb Memorial Day Contest; **Patchel**—"night train" *Frogpond* XXVII:1; **Pfleuger**—"spring again" *The Heron's Nest* VI:2, "the heat" *The Heron's Nest* VI:6; **Pizzarelli**—"the score keeper" *Frogpond* XXVII:3; **Porad**—"inserting a piece" *Frogpond* XXVII:3; **Proctor**—"garden path" *Presence* 23; **Reeves**—"red sunrise" *paper wasp* Winter 2004; **Ristic**—"this morning again" 38th A-Bomb Memorial Day Contest; **Robinson**—"Father's Day" *The Heron's Nest* VI:5, "first frost" *acorn* 12; **Romano**—"truant boys" *Modern Haiku* 35:3; **Russell**—"spring rain" Harold G. Henderson Haiku Contest 2004; **Sagan**—"our exchange student" 38th A-Bomb Memorial Day Contest; **Scott**—"summer 's end" *Presence* 22, "morning frost" *Hermitage* 1 & 2; **Shaw**—"a sudden warming" Kaji Aso Contest 2004; **Shimi**—"the crackle" *Frogpond* XXVII:3; **Shimizu**—"holidays over" *The Heron's Nest* VI:3; **Sohne**—"all that matters" *Haiku Canada Newsletter* XVII:2; **Spence**—"rain on my birthday" "using a peach" *Season of the Heart*; **Stanford**—"hands in prayer" *The Heron's Nest* VI:6; **Stevenson**—"class reunion" *The Heron's Nest* VI:7, "fireflies" *Modern Haiku*, "Oscar night" *GEPPO* XXIX:2; **Sterba**—"single living" *The Heron's Nest* VI:2; **Sternlieb**—"Moonpath Cottage" *Modern Haiku* 35:3; **Stoelting**—"boat dock" *The Heron's Nest* 35:1, "a phoebe's erratic flight" HPNC Haiku Contest 2004; **Story**—"Clack of the Rails" *xxx*; **Swede**—"Confessions over tea" *Frogpond* XXVII:1; **Tann**—"sitting" "quietly" "noh play" *dim sum* 2004/1; **Tarquinio**—"evening crickets" *The Heron's Nest* VI:10; **Tasker**—"On Broadway" *Presence* 23; **Tasnier**—"dressed again" *Presence* 23; **Tauchner**—"a new year" *Ko Autumn/Winter* 2004; **Tico**—

"my elbow slips off" *acorn* 13; **tripi**—"Fossil stone" *The Heron's Nest* VI:10; **Trumbull**—"sleepless night" *Haiku Canada Newsletter* XVII:1, "here and there" *Carrying Moonlight*; **Walker**—"laat night sirens" *acorn* 13; **Walsh**—"on display" Brady Senryu Contest; **Welch**—"tourists talking" HPNC Contest 2003, "moving day" *Frogpond* XXVII:1, morning chill *The Road*, "On Broadway" *Presence* 23, "The Hilltop Castle" HPNC Contest 2003; **Yarrow**—"remote village" *RAW NerVZ* IX:9; **Yoshimura**—"The Hilltop Castle" HPNC Contest 2003; **Young**—"autumn wind" *Frogpond* XXVII:2; **Yovu**—"leaves on the river" *The Heron's Nest* VI:5; **Zackowitz**—"autumn chill" *The Heron's Nest* VI:2; **Zambito**—"moving day" *bottle rockets* 10.

sources

Books

contemporary haibun 5 Jim Kacian, Bruce Ross & Ken Jones (eds.) (Red Moon Press, 2004)
Forefathers David Cobb (LeapPress, 2004)
The Road Ginka Biliarska (editor) (Bulgarian Haiku Club, 2004)
The Smell of Rust Margaret Chula (Katsura Press, 2003)
Season of the Heart Alan Spence (2004)

Periodicals

acorn (ed. A. C. Missias, P.O. Box 186, Philadelphia PA 19105, USA)
Blithe Spirit (ed. Colin Blundell, Longholm, East Bank, Wingland, Sutton Bridge, Spalding, Lincs, PE12 9YS, UK)
bottle rockets (ed. Stanford M. Forrester, PO Box 290691, Wethersfield CT 06129, USA)
frogpond (ed. Jim Kacian, PO Box 2461, Winchester VA 22604-1661, USA)
GEPPO (ed. Patricia Machmiller, 6116 Dunn Avenue, San Jose CA 95123, USA)
Haiku Canada Newsletter (ed. LeRoy Gorman, 51 Graham West, Napanee, Ontario K7R 2J6, Canada)
Hermitage (ed. Ion Codrescu, Str. Soveja, Nr. 25, Bl. V2, Sc. B, Apt. 31, Constantja, Romania)
Heron's Nest, The (ed. Christopher Herold, 816 Taft St., Port Townsend WA 98368, USA)
Hummingbird (ed. Phyllis Walsh, PO Box 96, Richland Center MN 55)
Ko (ed. Koko Kato, Nagoya Japan)
Mariposa (ed. D. Claire Gallagher, 864 Elmira Drive, Sunnyvale CA 94087-1229, USA)
Mayfly (ed. Randy M. Brooks, 3720 North Woodridge Dr, Decatur IL 62526, USA)
Modern Haiku (ed. Lee Gurga, Box 68, Lincoln IL 62656, USA)
paper wasp (ed. various, 7 Bellevue Terrace, St. Lucia, Queensland 406, Australia)
Presence (ed. Martin Lucas, 12 Grovehall Avenue, Leeds LS11 7EX, England, UK)
RAW NerVZ (ed. Dorothy Howard, 67 Court Street, Aylmer (QC) J9H 4M1, Canada)
Shadow Poetry Quill, no information
South by Southeast (ed. Steve Addis et. al.., RC Box 93, 28 Westhampton Way, Richmond VA 23173, USA)
Upstate Dim Sum (ed. Route 9 Haiku Group, PO Box 122, Nassau NY 12123, USA)
Yellow Moon (Ed. Beverley George, PO Box 37, Pearl Beach 2556 Australia)

Contests

A-Bomb Memorial Day Haiku Contest (38th Annual, 2004)
BHS James W. Hackett International Haiku Award 2003
Gerald Brady Senryu Contest 2004 (Haiku Society of America)
Haiku Poets of Northern California Haiku Contest 2004
Harold G. Henderson Haiku Contest (Haiku Society of America)
Kaji Aso Haiku Contest 2004 (Boston Haiku Society)

Online

Shiki Haiku Salon
Simply Haiku

the RMA editorial staff

Jim Kacian (1996) is a co-founder of the World Haiku Association, editor of *Frogpond*, and owner of Red Moon Press.

Ernest J. Berry (2002) is a newcomer to haiku who feels like an old hand. He defies the reaper by refusing to write his death haiku.

Tom Clausen (1996) half accepts change yet is always grateful for the constancy of nature, the seasons and haiku celebrating them.

David Cobb (2004), who had the nerve to co-found the British Haiku Society, currently is writing English grammar books for China.

Dee Evetts (2003) is a former HSA Secretary, and founder of the Spring Street Haiku Group. This is his second tenure with RMA..

Maureen Virginia Gorman (1997) believes her study of haiku is a perfect complement to her work as a professional counselor.

Carolyn Hall (2002) for four years co-editor of *Mariposa*, is trying hard to remain mindful of haiku moments.

A. C. Missias (2001) is the editor of *Acorn*, past columnist for *Frogpond*, and has placed in a few haiku competitions. What day job?

Kohjin Sakamoto (1997) a disciple of Kunio Tsukamoto, contemporary poetic giant, has won numerous poetry contests.

George Swede (2000) lives, works, writes in Toronto and lives, writes in San Antonio Tlayacapan, Mexico.

Max Verhart (2002) former president of the Dutch Haiku Circle, is now editor of *Vuursteen* (*Flint*), the oldest haiku journal in Europe.

RMA Editors-Emeritus: **Dimitar Anakiev** (2000-2001)**, Janice Bostok** (1996-2001), **Ellen Compton** (1996-2002), **Lee Gurga** (1998), **Yvonne Hardenbrook** (1996-8), **John Hudak** (1996-7), **H. F. Noyes** (1996-9), **Francine Porad** (1996), **Ebba Story** (1996), **Alan Summers** (2000-2004), **Jeff Witkin** (1996-2000).

the RMA process

DURING THE TWELVE MONTH PERIOD December 1, 2003 through November 30, 2004, over 2500 haiku and related works by over 1800 different authors have been nominated for inclusion in *tug of the current: The Red Moon Anthology 2004* by our staff of 11 editors from hundreds of sources from around the world. These sources are, in the main, the many haiku books and journals published in English, as well as the internet. Each editor is assigned a list of books and journals, but is free to nominate any work, from any source, s/he feels is of exceptional skill. In addition, the editor-in-chief is responsible for reading all of these sources, which ensures every possible source is examined by at least two nominating persons.

Editors may neither nominate nor vote for their own work.

Contest winners, runners-up and honorable mentions are automatically nominated.

When the nominating period concludes, all haiku and related works which receive nomination are placed (anonymously) on a roster. The roster is then sent to each of the judges, who votes for those works s/he considers worthy of inclusion. At least 5 votes (of the 10 judges, or 50%—the editor-in-chief does not have a vote at this stage) are necessary for inclusion in the volume. The work of editors must also receive at least 5 votes from the other 9 editors (55%) to merit inclusion.

The editor-in-chief then compiles these works, seeks permissions to reprint, and assembles them into the final anthology.